Christ's Centripetal Cross

Other books by Jeffrey Mackey

*Indicatives and Imperatives: An Introduction to
Biblical Ethics*

A Worship Manifesto

Christ's Centripetal Cross

Eschaton [poetry]

*A Diary of Three Decades
[A History of Grace Church, Utica, New York]*

Hidden Mirth

A Mirrored Surprise

Take Your Chants: A Worship Polemic

In Quest of the Holy: Theology in Synthesis

The Four Fold Gospel: A Pastoral Excursus

But I Repeat Myself

Worship as Evangelism

*He That Will Live Life
[A Daily Devotional on Leviticus]*

Books co-authored or contributed to by Jeffrey Mackey

Where Love and People Are [poetry]

*Prophet of Justice: Prophet of Life
[Essays on William Stringfellow]*

A Heart for the Future

Nudity and Christianity

Christ's Centripetal Cross

A Pastoral Theology of Crucifixion

Jeffrey A. Mackey

The Wilson Press ✦ New York

Scripture quotations, unless otherwise indicated, are from the personal translations of the author.

Mackey, Jeffrey Allen, 1952 –
Christ's Centripetal Cross – A Pastoral Theology of Crucifixion
1. Crosses 2. Jesus Christ – Crucifixion 3. Crucifixion 4. Holiness
I. Title

323.9'63

Cover design by J. Alex Whyte using Cover Creator, CreateSpace.com Painting of a Catskill Mountain, New York scene by an unknown artist.

Published by THE WILSON PRESS
Woodstock, New York
914.466.8367

This book is printed on acid-free paper that meets the American National Standards Institute Z39.48 standard. ∞

PRINTED IN THE UNITED STATES OF AMERICA

ISBN-13: 978-1456498870
ISBN-10: 1456498878

Table of Contents

Preface

It so happens that the remaining copies of the 1989 first edition were purchased by my eldest son, an Episcopal priest. He purchased them to use in group study at his parish, at that time, in Louisiana. Those who worked through the wee volume with Fr. Mackey were very complementary and thanked me profusely and profoundly when I visited there in 2008 right after their experience with the work. But what was humbling and spiritually gratifying was that *my son* praised the work and the part it played in his ministry with his congregation. I thought, "Thanks be to God for such a final use of this twenty-year-old attempt at simply expounding how the centrality of the Cross of Christ was pastorally meaningful in the life of those who sought to know Christ in real time and space.

The surprise came, when in the summer of 2010 my son called and said, "Dad, I need *Christ's Centripetal Cross* for my congregation here. Please do a bit of updating and have it reprinted by someone." I was in the midst of a Doctor of Philosophy dissertation, and in the process of readying my "A" Year pastoral commentary for press. And then I pulled out an original of *Christ's Centripetal Cross*. It continued to say what I believe the Canon of Holy Scripture says about the Cross, only in a synthetic and coalescing way. It is not academic: it is not intended to be. It is personal, spiritual, and "omni-applicable." Before the Cross of Christ can be held up as the hope of the world lost and searching for meaning, it must be by faith and conviction in the hearts of the people of God. For without the Cross the Resurrection is nothing. The late Hans Urs von Balthasar made this captivating and correct observation, *"Whoever removes the Cross and its interpretation by the New Testament from the center, in order to replace it, for example, with the social commitment of Jesus to the oppressed as a new center, no longer stands in continuity with the apostolic faith."*

A. B. Simpson, the Canadian Presbyterian who later, in New York City founded one of the greatest missionary-sending ministries in post-New Testament history, wrote in his diary on August 3, 1907: *"The cross of Christ generates the human heart. It puts a new nature in men, it makes the sinner automatically right, not driven by force or fear to keep some inexorable law, but drawn by the constraint of his own desire to do what God would have him to do and be what God would have him be; it puts a self acting principal in every man, which produces the fruit of righteousness just as naturally as a vine produces grapes and a rose produces fragrance.*

...It creates practical righteousness between man and man. It substitutes the Golden rule for the maxims of human policy, and teaches men to 'denying ungodliness and worldly lusts and to live soberly righteously and godly in this present evil world,' and leads men to desire a religion that can

8

change a pickpocket into an honest man and a cursing virago into a gentle saint.

...It elevates human society, gives freedom to the slave, sets women free from degradation and shame, builds every hospital that ever sheltered a sufferer, sends its red cross banner to the battlefield, and better still, teaches the nations to turn their swords into plowshares and study war no more."

I am of the conviction that the Cross of Christ is the place where grace abounds at its most infinite giving and where God invites at his most loving. Again, von Balthasar is spot on: *"Without a doubt, at the center of the New Testament there stands the Cross, which receives its interpretation from the Resurrection."*

And so, here in the summer in my study at Vicar's Grove in North Central Florida, I begin. There is no "saved document." It was typewritten prior to the days of personal computers. I may use some OCR at times, or I may merely sit and write. This gives time for thinking and meditation that mere editing cannot provide.

The various statements of gratitude in the original edition remain heart-felt though the people are far distant in time and space. My original dedication of the volume was to the wonderfully warm and sensitive evangelist, Dr. Bob Manderson. Bob ministered in every parish of which I was a pastor from 1974 through 1986. I miss him. He is happily helping to plan and prepare for the "Marriage Supper of the Lamb."

But I need to add a second dedication of this second edition of *Christ's Centripetal Cross: A Pastoral Theology of Crucifixion,* and that is to the Reverend Guy L. Mackey, DTheol. He is my son. He is a priest. He is very good at being both. I love you Father Mackey.

Jeffrey A. Mackey
The Feast of St Mary Magdalene, July 22, 2011
Vicars Grove – Melrose, Florida

Forward

I am indebted to a number of writers who have driven me to return to the theme of the Cross. Crucifixion was more common among Roman rule in Second Temple Judaism than any death penalty is in the Western World of 2011. It was taken as something that was, and though Hebrew Zealots wished to do away with the people and the practice, Rome's stranglehold kept that from happening.

It is essential that the reader keep in mind that these are either sermons or portions of sermons preached from 1985 through 2011. They may not always read as your latest novel reads. They are not intended to. Also it should be noted that I quote from others with regularity. Long ago I encountered the adage that, "He who does not quote will never be quoted." For what it is worth I state this.

Among the authors who have influenced my thinking are the unequalled A. W. Tozer, the one often termed, "The Twentieth Century Prophet." His book, *The Radical Cross,* is a posthumously published work that gathers up much of Tozer's understanding of cruciformity within the context of the Cross of Christ.

P. T. Forsyth's 1909 publication of *The Cruciality of the Cross* is indispensable to understanding the immovability of the Cross of Christ from the central place it holds in salvation history.

Others who have shaped my thinking here include, Dr. Steve Brown, Dr. Martin Lloyd-Jones, Dr. G. Campbell Morgan, Dr. John R. W. Stott, Dr. H. L. Goudge, C. S. Lewis, and many, many more. I owe a debt of gratitude to each of them, including my ecclesial authority, the Rt. Rev. Samuel Johnson Howard, Bishop of Florida, a man from whom I am learning to live in cruciformity. He has not only shaped my thinking but is shaping my heart, and making me a wee bit more like the Master.

Preliminary Essentials
The Cross as
The Cosmic Center

It is essential, unquestionably essential, that the Christian mind and heart revisit the fact that the cross is not an individual salvific act, producing a personal salvation experience, for a personal salvation in heaven when one dies. As true as these individual realities are, there is a fundamental fact of the cross, and that is, it is essentially the one and the only adequate, sufficient, and complete answer to the fallen cosmos in which all creatures live and which existed, prior to the cross, un-reconciled to God its creator. Every galaxy, every solar system, every planet, comet, asteroid, moon; and every creature found thereupon, be it animal, human, or to us, alien, is found in the cross as reconciled to God, and God to it and to them. It was precisely this truth that allowed Charles Wesley to pen these lyrics:

Arise, my soul, arise; shake off thy guilty fears;
The bleeding sacrifice in my behalf appears:
Before the throne my surety stands,
Before the throne my surety stands,
My name is written on His hands.

He ever lives above, for me to intercede;
His all redeeming love, His precious blood, to plead:
His blood atoned for all our race,
His blood atoned for all our race,
And sprinkles now the throne of grace.

Five bleeding wounds He bears; received on Calvary;
They pour effectual prayers; they strongly plead for me:
'Forgive him, O forgive,' they cry,
'Forgive him, O forgive,' they cry,
'Nor let that ransomed sinner die!'

The Father hears Him pray, His dear anointed One;
He cannot turn away, the presence of His Son;
His Spirit answers to the blood,
His Spirit answers to the blood,
And tells me I am born of God.

My God is reconciled; His pardoning voice I hear;
He owns me for His child; I can no longer fear:
With confidence I now draw nigh,
With confidence I now draw nigh,
And 'Father, Abba, Father,' cry.

"His blood atoned for all our race," is Wesley's proclamation of the one purpose of God, and that is the redemption of all, and that "my God is reconciled," is the assurance that now, all is well: the creation and all who are in it are reconciled, pardoned, and adopted in relationship to the Creator-Redeemer.

Until this is grasped, the cross is not grasped. It is central; it is the epicenter of reality upon which all of human history is hinged and whereupon all the creation finds its redemption and its purpose. St. Paul goes so far as to tell us that the very creation, "groans for its final deliverance" [Romans 8:20-21]. One anonymous writer puts it this way: "All of creation is waiting in a mysterious way to be set free and to obtain a glorious liberty together with all the children of God."

This centrality of the cross reveals the singular purpose of God in his creative and redemptive actions. Seeing this, one is confident along with the Apostle Paul that, *"God has imprisoned all in disobedience* [the result both of the Fall and of each person's own sinning] *so that he may be merciful to all"* [Romans 11:32]. The attributes of God: mercy, grace, love, compassion, each alone and all together, outweigh the temporary actions of God: anger, wrath, change of mind, etc. The cross is the declaration that the God of holy attribution wins, through Christ, everything that was lost through Adam. The singular purpose of God is to reclaim, through redemption, all that was lost in the Fall. French author Charles Pe´guy, a

15

longtime agnostic and antagonist to Christianity wrote, "A religion which has decided to acquiesce in the eternal lostness of brothers is fundamentally egoistic with regard to salvation, and this is basically 'bourgeois' and 'capitalistic.'"

The cross must also be seen in all its splendor as to its availability and power to the whole race and not merely to "me." The Romantic Period [mid-Eighteenth Century and through the Industrial Revolution] brought a Christian literature and a Christian hymnody [and Gospel music along with it] to a fundamentally self-centered approach to the redemption completed on the cross.

This cross, because of this radical centrality is not a cross of preparation for the after-life, but rather is the answer to eternal life which begins in the temporal and is everlasting. N. T. Wright warns, "The worry about the afterlife and the precise qualifications for it, which have so characterized Western Christianity, especially (it seems) since the Black Death, and which have shaped and formed Western readings (both Catholic and Protestant) of the New Testament, do not loom so large in the literature of Paul's contemporaries." Rather, "The tide which was carrying all Israel along in the time of Jesus and Paul was the tide of hope, hope that Israel's God would act once more and this time do it properly, that the promises made to Abraham and his family would at last come true, that the visions of the prophets who foretold a coming restoration would find their ultimate fulfillment. What we in the Western world have come to see as the 'individual' hope, and indeed the individual life of faith, piety or virtue, *found their place within that."*

So the cross eliminates "me-ism" and therefore the majority of Western (especially American) forms of Christianity. It is not what I think or feel that is important, rather it is what God has done in Christ through the Incarnation, Passion, Death, Burial, Resurrection and Ascension, that possess the immoveable center.

Chapter One
Why a "Pastoral Theology?"
An Introduction

"The cross cannot be defeated, for it is defeat."
                                    G. K. Chesterton

"In the cross is the height of virtue; in the cross is the perfection of sanctity. There is no health of the soul nor hope of eternal life but in the cross."
                                    Thomas A Kempis

"In all our actions, when we come in or go out, when we dress, when we wash, at our meals, before retiring to sleep, we make on our foreheads the sign of the cross. These practices are not committed by a formal law of Scripture, but tradition teaches them, custom confirms them, faith observes them."
                                    Quintus Tertullian

"[At the cross] God's controversy with man draws to a head in the unity of reconciliation, which solves the tragedy of guilt and grief."

P. T. Forsyth

"Too many adjustments have been made to (get the greatest number of people to become Christians), until the most important part of the gospel itself has been overlooked."

John Fischer

Any theology or doctrine unmoored from day-to-day life is merely academic [that is why the incubation theory of seminary education is grossly misleading]; may prove all types of things; may be right or wrong. It is, unquestionably, divorced from what you and I need when each day begins and through which time we must live. I need a theology which will "pastor" me through real life. If it is not applicable and available and effective there, it is not worth the paper on which it is written. Therefore for theology to be more than a science [which it was considered all through the Middle Ages and for a long time thereafter] it must be applied – it must take truth and make it applicable in our lives. The manifold things that wrangle for our attention in the 21st century are vicious. They play to the world, the flesh, and the devil. And if, as we believe and teach, the cross is irremovably central to our faith, our spiritual life and our secular life, any theology of the cross, by which we live, must, therefore, be a pastoral or practical theology. Such a theology takes the Biblical realities of the cross, and applies them, by grace, to our daily engagements with antagonistic principalities and powers.

Many significantly large and potent words are attached to the theology of the cross, and we will encounter them throughout this work. But I must invite my reader onward, for, I believe I have been able, to some small, yet beneficial degree, to make those concepts understandable, at least to myself. I trust you are helped by them as well. Von Balthasar speaks again to this when he writes: "*If God wishes*

21

to reveal the love that he harbors for the world, this love has to be something that the world can recognize, in spite of, or in fact in, its being wholly other."

So we venture into the theology of wood, but not just any wood, the wood of crucifixion, and not just any crucifixion, but the crucifixion of the one who is maintained in Christian orthodox theology as the *theanthropic* being: the God-man. This cross belongs to none other than God the Son, the Incarnate one who benignly invaded human history according to the Evangelists, and who, through his life, death, burial, resurrection and ascension, made unparalleled eternal provision for those who were not reconciled to God. In this cross, both God and humanity are reconciled. Each side is reconciled with the other. The God-man brings God and man together in nothing less than complete reconciliation.

My God is reconciled,
His pardoning voice I hear;
He owns me for his child,
I can no longer fear.
In confidence I now draw nigh,
And "Abba, Father, Abba," cry.

Charles Wesley

Again, Von Balthasar would agree. *"If one does away with the fact of the Resurrection, one also does away with the Cross, for both stand and fall together, and one would then have to find a new center for the whole message of the gospel."* If we do away with any part of the work of Christ Jesus, we have pulled a thread that undoes the entirety of the truth of the cross.

One final thought of this pastoral or practical theology of the cross. As humans we need access to forgiveness, enablement, and encouragement. These are provided through the atoning work of the cross. *"For we do not have a high priest who is unable to sympathize with our weaknesses, but one who in every respect has been tempted as we are yet without sin."* [Hebrews 4:15]. We have a priest who knows us as we are. He has been here and the place is not foreign to him. This is theology at its best: God Incarnate, now the God-man at the right hand of the Father. As it has been said or sung for two-thousand years, Christ is victim, Christ is priest.

Again the unknown writer of Hebrews gives us the practicality of this God-man in glory: *"Now the point in what we are saying is this: we have such a high priest, one who is seated at the right hand of the Majesty in heaven, a minister in the holy places..."* [Hebrews 8:1,2a]. This is sufficient evidence to show us how utterly practical and pastoral the theology of the cross really is. Remove it from the horizon of Christian history and you destroy Christian history. The cross and everything that goes with it is woven into the fabric of the provision of God for his creatures who were irredeemably unable to provide for themselves. This is a pastoral theology of the cross.

A. B. Simpson, the late Victorian missiologist wrote spot on doctrinally when he wrote the words to a great Advent hymn:

There is a name, to Jesus given,
His matchless love its accents tell;
For it declares, he is my brother,
And this his name: Emmanuel.

The Lord by angels worshipped yonder,
Has stooped to earth with men to dwell.
Incarnate God, and man forever,
Our own beloved, Emmanuel.

Chapter Two
The Serious Nature of the Cross

Our Lady stood beside the cross
A little space apart,
And when she heard our Lord cry out,
A sword went through her heart.
                              Hillary Belloc

"Christ's cross is such a burden as sails are to a ship
and wings to a bird."
                              Samuel Rutherford

"In the cross of Christ the excess of man is met by the
excess in God, excess of evil is mastered by excess of
love."
                              Louis Bourdaloue

"You were there when they crucified my Lord."
                              Adapted

"Most crosses we encounter are harmless. They dangle from an ear or wrist or lie in the nape of a pretty neck. The perch atop buildings or adorn the interior walls of our places of worship. The cross has become and ornament, a religious symbol mellowed by sentimental value."

John Fischer

There is a stark seriousness about the cross. After all, we are speaking of a method of human execution. This is not a popular subject. It is so strange a way for God to gain victory over the creation, and stranger still that it has been the symbol of the faith of Christians for over 2,000 years. Go into any jewelry store and they will show you all kinds of crosses you can wear, usually on a chain or as a pin. It is alleged that one man, wanting to purchase a cross for his wife, was asked by the proprietor of the establishment, "Would you be interested in a plain cross, or one with the little man on it?" So secularized is the Western world that the cross, even historically or culturally understood is missed entirely by the world whizzing past at breakneck speed. Everyone has forgotten who that "little man" was. And in forgetting, they have distanced themselves from the biggest man who ever has or ever will exist; the God-man, Jesus Christ.

There is a deteriorating interest given to the words of God when they relate to something painful- when they do not fit into our culture of ease and comfort. The pleasure orientation of Western culture [which is rapidly being exported to Eastern culture and will spell its demise as well], makes the serious nature of any faith system suspect when it comes to post-modernity. We want spirituality, but only the spirituality that gives us what we have discovered our "needs" to be. Sensationalism, particularly in Western Christianity has completely overwhelmed the concept that the revelation of God may require something of us, and that something is a seriousness which must be in place before the sensation can be truly Christian. Subjectivity in the realm of the spiritual has overtaken any objective revelation and has thrown the church into the entertainment business instead of into the business of the cross. At one point churches had such things as catechisms, daily prayers, and in the church building proper, there were often "mourners' benches." Now we have recreated church so that it reflects the opposite of what Kierkegaard wrote when he commented that we should, metaphorically, view worship as a dramatic presentation. The audience is not the people in the pews or seats, but rather is God, himself. The believing congregants are the players, and the priest or pastor is merely the prompter. Who imagines this today? Recently this author had a man of good standing in his parish, visit the office to inform him that, "I come to church to feel good, and I want music that makes me feel good." Maybe he wants more than a true church can offer. For the bad news of the cross precedes the good news of resurrection. Both foci are necessary, but in that prescribed order. There is no glory that comes before degradation. The words of Christ, "It is finished," must always lead the procession which ends dramatically and victoriously with, "He is risen!"

The church and its individual members must find again that the power we so lust after spiritually, came *after* the cross. The resurrection is necessarily a following act. Before we get to joy we must first know the reality of passion. But joy does follow: not the giddy happiness of junior high students awash in emotive vacuity over some new gadget. But joy, deep joy, which has little parallel with modernity's or with all of post-modernity's sensationalistic happiness.

One is intrigued by the way adults in chronological age, seem to remain teeny-boppers in spiritual age when it comes to the cross and to the worship of the One who made the cross what it is. Modernity murdered worship, and the only way to return to a Biblically sanctioned corporate worship is through a time-travel backward to the worship of the ancient church. The wonder, awe, mystery, questions, paradoxes, will all give to the contemporary seeker the thrills they want and need, only they will be the thrills of experiencing the crucified and risen Christ, and not some social construct of him.[1]

The decisive is waning in the Christian West, and therefore Christianity is waning in the Christian West. While there has been a dearth of the preaching of radical grace since the Reformation [in evangelical churches it was what we didn't do or did do that mattered to our salvation's security and in the liberal churches it only mattered what you did there was little or no emphasis on knowing God and the vitality and dynamic of Holy Spirit] there is now only grace and it is left up to any person to define that grace in any manner they wish.

According to Christopher Benton in *Christianity Today,* [December 2010] Christians in

---

[1] The author deals extensively with this in the 2010 Blackfriar Books release of his *Take Your Chants: A Worship Polemic.*

the West are, "Addicted to novelty, and are therefore seduced to forget the wisdom of an Israelite King, 'There is nothing new under the sun' [Ecclesiastes 1:9]." When Christians, "rank their relationship with God above what God did, does, and will do in Jesus Christ, they make better German Romantics than biblical disciples....the person of Christ becomes increasingly impersonal and the Christian experience becomes increasingly unchristian."

Rather than the cross confronting us with the serious nature of our condition and the serious provision of grace that redeems us from that condition, we remain a Christianity that is filled with a, "consumer spirituality."

In this society, then, the cross becomes unpopular in the least, and unarguably countercultural at its most defining point. A mass media Christianity, unfortunately fails at too many points to delineate.

The question of the cross, then becomes, "What do we give to a God who gives everything?" The only possible answer is ourselves. His cross: our salvation; ourselves, his reward.

Chapter Three
The Cross: Its Depth and Simplicity

"The Cross of Christ is the most revolutionary thing ever to appear among men."

A. W. Tozer

"The theology of the cross is not restricted to the sphere of subjectivity; but it is utterly practical in orienting a person with the right approach to reality."

Carl A. Braaten

"The cross shows little regard for relevancy in any age. While each generation tries to manifest its own culture, the cross seems hardly to care. At any point in history, at any place on this planet, the death of Christ, like the lines of the cross itself, runs perpendicular to the flow of culture. The cross is shocking, arresting, out of step, out of time...and yet for all time."

John Fischer

"God is a god who works through contraries."
                                    Peter L. Steinke

Over recent decades, two particular books have drawn this author's attention, and the attention of others to the nature of the Gospel of Jesus Christ. In seeking to evangelize the unbelievers in our midst, we have often overlooked the teachings of these two volumes, but for used bookstores, would be lost to us because of their age. They are not large volumes, nor is there anything in the bindings that would draw a booklover to take a second look at them. They possess no rare book value, and the copies in this author's library came from no one's particular collection as far as he can tell.

Nonetheless, there has been a drawing in of all my thinking over and over again as I take these from the shelves and give them my time. I surmise the original draw to these volumes would be their titles. They are out of place with my other books on evangelism, mission, church growth, and developmental theology, successful Christian living, and on and on. The titles, at least, are out of place with the majority. The titles suggest something radically different than the average run-of-the-mill "how to" book on growing churches.

Each book is out of print. The first is *The Reproach of the Gospel,* and its companion volume, *The Faith that Must Offend.*[2] Each book grapples with certain aspects of New Testament faith which is almost unanimously overlooked in the post-modern, "try-it-you'll-like-it" invitation in so many Christian

---

[2] *The Reproach of the Gospel* is by James. F. H. Peile, MA, published in 1907, and the second by Joseph McCulloch published in 1942.

circles. I began to wonder if these authors were on to something; something missing in the contemporary mode of evangelism; not something in place of the contemporary, but rather the paradox and counter-balance to what everyone is doing now that, "seems to work." [One finds after decades of Biblical and theological study, that any theology without a paradox tied to its side is a theology devoid of wholeness.].

John R. W. Stott in his unequalled tome, *The Cross of Christ,* comes to press and reminds its readers of this Gospel reproach and the offense, particularly of the cross when it is taken seriously and viewed as reality.

One could only pray that the church is on the precipice of jumping headlong into the joyous abyss of a reawakened interest in and attachment to the cross of Christ. Carl Braaten writes that there needs to be a renewed interest in, "the kind of suffering that comes from bearing the cross of Christ." And it is this suffering, this enmity with the world systems, that the church of the 20th century lost. In a head-long rush to get along, it has gone along. The methods of the world have not become the methods of the church, they have become the message of the church. Marshall MacLuhan was not far off when he coined the phrase, "The medium is the message," back in 1964. One might ask if there is anything of the cross in contemporary "prosperity gospel" messages; any cross in the current "mass counseling from the pulpit," movements; any cross in the "signs and wonders" doctrines which are taking over churches of all stripes at an incalculable rate. But could there be "a still small voice" trying to be heard amidst the cacophonous clamor of embarrassingly vacuous Christianity?

As the 21st century dawned and the first generation of televangelists approached their farewell to this earth, most of them turned ministry over to their children, who were, without question, called to the exact ministries as the parents. In practically every case, with a few exceptions, the passing of the baton has been an embarrassing series of dead ends; if not for them, for those of us who happen to stop the remote on a station featuring their broadcast. I will do all within my power to hold back on the mentioning of names and "ministries," but the downward spiral is conspicuous. It is conspicuous, because no matter what the elder statesman or woman held, there was still something, however infinitesimal of the cross in their work and message. The cross today is jewelry and decoration; formerly it was an offense and a reproach.

So one begins to approach the cross with the contemporary question, is it possible that this cross which was so very much part of the actual history of the man Jesus, has something relevant to say to the human heart and to the church today? I have come to believe that it does. The cross speaks to the person who has the honesty, authenticity, and integrity to listen. As the cross is the emblem of the church, the rallying point of believers, the cross is also the reward of those who seek Christ. The cross is the immediate business, not only of the religious--the clergy, but of every average Christian.

In this cross, the cross of Christ, is found the answer to the striking contrast between the lives of Christians who throw their total dependency upon it, and those who live according to rules they profess to accept and proclaim they have received from that cross. The cross is nothing if it is not the death of the law and the total, complete, everlasting, and dynamic revelation of the unrestricted grace of God. This cross needs to be taken off the walls of monasteries, convents, parochial schools, and churches and be placed once again in heart, so that it is placed in homes and offices and vehicles and factories. The cross needs to be placed again in the every day secular world. It is the cross that sanctifies what otherwise is purely secular.

The first realization must be that the cross of Christ, so central to the history of redemption, and the cross of the Christian, cannot be separate. They may not be conceived of separately, thought of separately, or seen separately; the Christian's cross is the cross of Jesus Christ. When Jesus called men to follow him carrying their own crosses, it must be remembered that they went in the direction he went, they followed the course he chose, and they were known by the company they were found in. Though each had his own cross to bear, each individual cross was defined by the one who imposed its weight upon those who bore it. It was as C. S. Lewis writes, "the weight of glory."

The Christian life is always a life under the cross. J.B. Phillips rightly assesses, "Until the final curtain falls, the church or the individuals who compose the church, make no real progress unless they live under the cross."

Another consideration is that the world, in no way, understands the cross-bearing work of the believer in Jesus Christ. To hold out hope that there can be an understanding, acceptance, consideration, admiration, on the part of the world, toward those who have taken up the cross is to misunderstand the radical nature of Christian discipleship. That which does not bow the knee can in no way understand that which does. Darkness has no fellowship with light. That does not mean that the believer is taken out of the world but rather that the believer is thrust into the darkness of the world to remind it and its inhabitants that they are under the redemption purchased by Jesus Christ.

Phillips evaluates the situation in this manner: "to those who are outside the pale of the church of God...there often seems something pathetic and even ridiculous in the Christian's proclaiming of the cross."

To attempt to erase this repugnance is to dilute the true sense of cross-bearing. It is categorically impossible for the church of Christ and the cross of Christ to be morph into something they are not, merely to simplify religion so that there would be nothing offensive and no one to offend. It seems that in the Christian West, things Christian are being de-emphasized. But the Eastern religions,

Hinduism, Buddhism, and Islam, dare not be offended. Say nothing about a Jew or you will be called anti-Semitic. But say all you want about the Christian and his cross and he dare not respond. Maybe that's just how Jesus wanted it?

The apostle Paul reminded the Corinthian believers that "the natural mind receives not the things of the Holy Spirit, for they are spiritually discerned." He found the preaching of the cross foolishness to some, a stumbling block to others, and the very symbol of redemption to others. Even with these caveats, the preaching of the cross was Paul's only preaching. It was his only boast.

Another consideration of the cross is that it affects a far deeper change in a person than "all the high thinking and clever talk could ever do." The cross takes everything a person is or has and recreates them; makes them completely and entirely new. Whereas all the moral philosophers and psychiatric insiders may appear eminently successful in taking poor ones and making them rich; bad ones and making them good; dirty ones and making them clean; depressed ones and making them upbeat; the cross is the only reality that can intervene in the affairs of men and make the dead live! The Apostle John brings to our mind in I John 2:2, *"Christ is the propitiation for our sins; and not for ours only, but for the sins of the whole world."* This is not only personal change, this change possesses cosmic significance. This cross on which propitiation was made [read: atonement] is radical and powerfully unique and benign.[3] This cross produces illimitable change.

H. L. Goudge, father of the famous novelist Elizabeth Goudge, was an outstanding British pastoral theologian. He writes of the cross of Christ; *"Satan was the prince of the world once, and he rules still in the 'sons of disobedience." But the crucial judgment has taken place; the prince of the world has been cast out; and Christ the victor is drawing, though not dragging, all men unto himself. What tarries is not the victory but the full manifestation of the victory; and even that will come soon enough....the Lord's own victory is already complete....the end of the conflict is in sight."[4]*

Might it be, with all of the church's planning, programming, conferencing, retreating, etc, that somewhere along the line has been lost the true center-the true retreat? Is it possible, in the least, that the Church has adopted and adapted the secular, fallen worldview as it has schemed for and developed programs for growth while thinking it was discipling believers? If a committee is effective and a job description up-to-date, do we then guarantee spiritual Cross-centeredness? Exactly how do we measure unquantifiable variables? Do the best of managerial and contemporary "leadership" tools differ at all from, "it seemed good to the Holy Spirit and to us?"

---

[3] Benign, "good-natured; kind; favorable; beneficent; beneficial.
[4] H. L. Goudge, *Glorying in the Cross,* London: Hodder & Stoughton, 1940, p.38,

The Church and the individual believer must consciously place something of the cross of Christ in the mind: a cross which has effected a victory which is being manifest right now in the lives of men and women worldwide.

Think no thoughts directly; allow thought to always move through the filter of the Cross. John Bowring penned the words that have become lost to a generation of creative novelty in Christian music. But his words are the only way a centripetal cross can orient a person.

> *In the cross of Christ, I glory,*
> *Towering o'er the wrecks of time;*
> *All the light of sacred story*
> *Gather 'round its head sublime.*

With the heart and mind so set, one can own *The Reproach of the Gospel* and *The Offense of the Cross* with a hitherto unknown humility which will keep one cruciform. The deeply mystical Roman Catholic priest and poet, Daniel Barrigan hit it clearly when he wrote, *"To be a Christian, you've got to look good on wood."*

Chapter Four
Christ's Centripetal Cross

"The plain fact is that the Christian must accept life at the hands of the Father."

J. B. Phillips

"Until we have learned that no individual, church or nation can play tricks with God, that he has his own way and time of doing things, he will wait, that he may be gracious; and blessed are they who turn away from Egypt, with their chariots and horsemen, and wait for him.

J. Gregory Mantle

"Because we lost our idea of God, nothing has meant anything very much, or anything has meant nothing at all."

Joseph McCulloch

*"There is a great difference between realizing, "On the act cross he was crucified **for** me," and "On that cross I am crucified **with** him." The one aspect brings us deliverance from **sin's condemnation,** the other from **sins power.**"*

Richard Halverson

"Hardly ever does he [Jesus] refer to his passion without speaking of the glory to which it leads....[the] Lord regards the conflict before him as a personal conflict between himself and the unseen powers of evil and thinks of himself as the one who attacks. But to attack Satan means to attack the system and the persons in whom Satan is incarnate, and that is what the Lord did. Our Lord was not a victim suffering from unprovoked cruelty; he laid down his life for his friends in a frontal attack upon the whole system which kept them in bondage."

H. L. Goudge

The cross is the center point of Biblical, Christian faith. Though often, through neglect, or more likely embarrassment, overlooked, it is nonetheless the thematic center around which the drama of New Testament history unfolds. It is necessary to revisit the cross; it is necessary to re-emphasize the cross; it is necessary to reorient the church from the perspective of the cross, for in the cross is the foundation of Christian faith: history, heritage, and hope.

J. I. Packer, low church Protestant Anglican captures this in his words that the cross, "is a distinguishing mark of the world-wide evangelical fraternity; it takes us to the very heart of the gospel." John R. W. Stott, an Anglican of parallel conviction to Packer laments the relative lack of evangelical books which deal directly with the cross of Christ. And this is written in his 1980s release of *The Cross of Christ!* Stott is one of the best reads on the cross, though scholarly and a bit dense at times, yet nonetheless, one of the best places to go when one finishes this work. His is theology, mine, pastoral theology. The difference may be miniscule, but there is a difference. Pastoral theology does not exist without a, "therefore." There is always application in pastoral theology. And so we see how the cross, thrust into the life of a person or group of persons, will swirl everything in predestined chaos around the only organizing reality in the entire cosmos, the cross of Christ.

Not only should the believer regain appreciation for the cross, but along with such appreciation must find the centrality, the power, the indispensability of the cross of Christ. This is necessary to understand the grace and love of God even at a rudimentary level. Again H. L. Goudge does us a great service by writing: *"The Lord did not go up to Jerusalem to preach the Kingdom of God....He went up, not to preach, but to judge – to attack and overthrow the kingdom of evil, knowing that he would die in the conflict, but that by dying he would rise to his throne."*

In light of New Testament history and revelation, the cross is seen as the ultimate and only transforming object in world history. All other actions, reactions, and events pale into insignificance when lifted next to this cross. The cross orients. It is the hub of the wheel of history, where, if the spokes do not meet at the hub, they are out of sync-completely valueless or unnecessary. It is our Lord who makes the cross and the cross that makes our Lord. Read backward the cross is the remaking of the manger's humble wood and read forward the cross is the throne from which the Prince of Peace reigns!

The very dating of history and its absolute course is changed from a garbage heap outside the gates of Jerusalem circa 30AD. John R. W. Stott declares: "It gives us a new, worshipping relationship to God, a new and balanced understanding of ourselves, a new incentive to give ourselves in mission, a new love for our enemies, and a new courage to face the perplexities of suffering."

Again and again we are drawn to the words of the Savior recorded in John 12:32, "and I, if I be lifted up, will draw all men to myself." There is a centripetal universality of the provisional dynamic of the cross. Jesus, in prophesying his own death by crucifixion is declaring that it is a purposeful death, a death for every person. This is, however, far from being an empty or hopeless message of death; it is the magnetic and hopeful message of life, of increase, of redemption. No greater text in the New Testament Scriptures gives us the foundation for an understanding of the universal provision of salvation for every person. It is universal provision for humanity is elect in the Son. There is no room at all for a theology which asks, "Who are the elect?" The question is moot.

No doubt Peter, the sometimes pesky Apostle, had these words of his Lord in mind when he wrote, "the Lord is...not willing that any should perish, but that all should come to repentance" [I Peter 3:9]. It is this cross which attracts, which draws, which invites. No "limited atonement" cross could be the work of the benign, loving God of Scripture. There is no repellant intent in the cross, there is only invitation.

Many have experienced centriugal forces when as children we played on the merry-go-round, or when we swung precariously around poles, causing ourselves to become dizzy or disoriented. Centrifugal forces pulled us outward, but centripetal forces drew us in, and all the more as the speed increased, though we never sensed them.

There are other illustrations of centripetal force, as when a power-source is introduced into the center of matter, such as a mixer into a bowl of cake batter; a stirring rod into a can of unmixed paint; or even a magnet into the distributed iron filings. Grandmothers have been watched for ages as they made swirl cakes with different color batters which drew to the center as they were stirred. And many have watched as a base paint color is tinted with just the right amount of tint color and then stirred with swirls moving inward.

Scripture is clear, that, no one can "come to me, unless the Father who sent me draw him..." and without confusing the Father, Son, and Holy Spirit, we see the Father and the Son in this Scripture, and the very drawing is the person of Holy Spirit. Salvation is a Trinitarian power, and a Trinitarian declaration of the will of God. So by the cross of crucifixion, God draws all to himself. Though all persons do not come [obviously], the "lifting up" of Jesus is the unanimous action of invitation on God's part. It is the Triune God making a provision to all humankind. To seek to limit its applicability or availability or its universality is to do injustice to a just God who, through his holiness and righteousness has acted in grace toward all. Who can rightly question God's right to redeem all if he so pleases? Certainly the cruciform provision is there drawing everyone to the Father through Christ.

One is then drawn out of himself into Christ. The cross, thrust into the world, invites "whosoever will" to come and find provided, their salvation.

This centripetal cross draws me out of my own insufficiencies into his security as well. Pride and egoism are centrifugally cast off and the naked self is drawn into the abundance and supernal wonders of the God of salvation found at the center. The hymn writer captured this with the words, "my only hope is found in Jesus' righteousness."

Over the centuries, a myriad of doctrinal creeds have enveloped the concept of security. Legitimate and illegitimate adjectives have dwarfed the magnitude of security itself. Our Lord's Disciples found their security in looking at and being with him, not by looking within themselves and casting worrisome eyes on their present circumstances.

The World War II survivor/evangelist, Corrie ten Boom reminds us of this in her little triple line poem:

Look around and be distressed;
Look within and be depressed;
Look at God and be at rest!

The cross of Christ is the clarion call out of my own security into the security embraced by present faith and trust in Christ. Security is not a doctrine but a relationship: a cruciform relationship. There is no place for pride, self-esteem, self-righteousness. There is place only for Christ. The sinner exchanges the sinful self for the saved self which is nothing less than the Christ-life.

Again, A. B. Simpson writes in his Gospel hymn of this exchange:

Once it was the blessing, now it is the Lord;
Once it was the feeling, now it is his Word;
Once his gift I wanted, now the Giver own!
Once I sought for healing, now himself alone.

Once 'twas painful trying, now 'tis perfect trust;
Once a half-salvation, now the uttermost;
Once 'twas ceaseless holding, now he holds me fast,
Once was constant drifting, now my anchor's cast.

This cross draws me out of myself, into his worship and his service. The redeemed live a life of gracious debt in light of gratuitous salvation. James Montgomery Boice expounds the believer's place in the service of Christ by writing, "The yoke placed upon the shoulders of a farm animal enables it to work. The yoke of Christ, placed upon the shoulders of his followers, undoubtedly has a similar purpose in their lives. It means we are hitched to his team or enlisted in his service. We are in his army, builders of his temple, evangelists for his gospel, ambassadors for his kingdom."

The cross links a person's salvation to his involvement in Christ's bidding to follow him. The cross, when thrust into the center of one's life draws all past, present, and subsequent activity to the center: the cross itself. This centripetal nature of the cross frames one's priorities in concentric circles with one's own person spiritual life at the first ring circling the cross. In the cross, the individual will is sanctified. It is no longer personally possessed-it is Christ possessed. The will of the Crucified One becomes primary. An Anglican Bible translator puts it like this: "For as little (as the) church has moved forward, it has been inescapably *the church under the cross*. Whenever we read reliable church history, whether of a thousand years ago or of today, whether in this country or in the far-off places of the earth, the same patterns of the cross repeat themselves. They are quite simply, the patterns of human life lived under the direction of the Holy Spirit."

And what is true of the church is also true of the individuals who make up the church. Cross centered thinking, willing, feeling, and doing, takes one out of himself and into Christ's service.

"Not my will, but yours be done," is more than mere rhetoric. "Lord, what would you have me to do?" is not an empty question uttered by a man to break deafening silence! Yet never in the history of the church has there been greater apathy toward doing the work of the ministry in Christ's way and with Christ's methodology. It is vogue to speak much of lay ministry on the one hand and yet on the other to pay the minister and expect the professional staff to do all Christian service. Christian service is for those who have the cross as the center of their lives.

Finally the cross of Christ draws me out of myself and into his similitude. Not only does Jesus draw all persons to himself, he draws all of every person to himself. The New Testament defines the believer in terms of that believer's behavior or their likeness to Christ. The writings of the apostle Paul are plain, equivocal, and quite forceful. Colossians 1:28 speaks of every man being presented perfect in

Christ. This is a work of grace in the life of a person who by grace, works the works of grace. Likewise, Romans 8:29 states that the predestined goal of the Christian life is Christ-likeness. My greatest appeal to the world is the appeal I make when Christ is seen in me. My greatest speech is built around the theme of Christ. The greatest form my growth can take is in the mold of Christ. And any sweet fragrance of life is found in the fragrance of Christ.

The cross, though personally enriching, filling, satisfying, and meeting every human need, is, nonetheless, uncompromisingly demanding in this regard. All of my goals, loves, desires, possessions are now his-remolded, remade, redefine in terms of similitude to my master. This is the message of the cross.

C. S. Lewis challenged his readers onward to such Christ likeness when he wrote: "when he said, 'Be perfect,' he meant it. He meant that we must go in for the full treatment. It is hard; but this sort of compromise we are all hankering after is harder-in fact, it is impossible. It may be hard for an egg to turn into a bird; it would be a jolly sight harder for it to learn to fly while remaining an egg. We are all eggs at present. And we cannot go on indefinitely just being in ordinary decent egg. We must be hatched ….

"If we let him-for we can prevent him, if we choose-he will make the feeblest and filthiest of us into a god or goddess, a dazzling, radiant, immortal creature pulsating all through with such energy and joy and wisdom and love as we cannot now imagine, a bright stainless mirror which reflects back to God perfectly (though of course, on a smaller scale) his own boundless power and delight and goodness. The process will be long and in parts very painful; but that is what we are in for. Nothing less."

Chapter Five
The Cross of Christ Himself

"Our Lord, who saved the world through the cross, will only work for the good of souls through the cross."

Madeleine Sophie Barat

"That there was no room in the inn was symbolic of what was to happen to Jesus. The only place there was room for him was on the cross."

William Barclay

"The cross of Christ does not make God love us; it is the outcome and measure of his love for us."

Andrew Murray

"Christ on our cross is the way Calvary really reads. For he died for us - in our place. We, then, are debtors. Strange that so often we act like we owe nothing."

C. Neil Strait

"Jesus Christ's death on a cross does not have to be ratified by anyone. It does not have to be understood to be true. The gospel does not have to move me emotionally before it can save me. The Son of God died on a real wooden cross on a rocky hillside in human history for the sins of the world. You and I were not there to see it or hear it, but God saw it, and therein lies its primary significance."

John Fischer

The cross of Christ was not unlike the crosses of other common criminals of the first century Roman Empire. There was an across-the-board negative reaction when we read, "and there they crucified him" [Matthew 27:35]. There is something unanimous among the crucified, possibly the ubiquitous curse put upon them by God and recorded in Deuteronomy 21:23, "for he who is hanged on a tree is accursed of God." Literally, "the one hung on a tree is the curse of God." So in intent, and in surface reality, the cross of our Lord Jesus Christ was common, profane, and completely utilitarian.

However, there is something of that cross which distinguishes it from all others. There is that notion that sets it apart, separates it, and makes it different. This is the first cross in the history of what would become the Christian faith. Though offensive, it is nonetheless embraced. Though it represents the reproach of the Gospel, yet it becomes the very symbol of that same Gospel.

Nowhere else in the religions of humankind is there such a profound and marked paradox as there is in the shameful cross becoming a symbol of greatness through humility and power through weakness. The cross of Christ becomes the glory of God revealed in human life and death. The cross, this tool of demeaning human death even more than it demeans itself had and has become from earliest Christian history until today, a wonderful and steady gathering place for men and women who would find God through the Son. Nowhere else is there such a symbol found. Never has anything so dreadfully and irredeemably lowly become that which is the very salvation mark of the world.

As we try our best to look objectively at the cross of Christ, there are a number of factors which seem to define its existence and its effects.

First, the cross of Christ is perilously dangerous. Even our Lord Jesus Christ himself was confronted with these spiritual dangers. The skeptics and the scoffers shouted unmercifully and unrelentingly to him, "You who destroy the temple and rebuild it in three days, save yourself. If you are God's Son come down from the cross" [Matthew 27:40]. There is a very real sense in which he, "could have called ten thousand angels, to destroy the world, and set him free," but these are dangers, temptations and not the yielding. Jesus faced such dangers on the cross and the dangers are still present for any cruciform saint, since the servant is not higher than his master. Each and every follower of Jesus is faced at times with perilous spiritual dangers if he is serious about the crucified life. There is the ever present tempting danger of abandonment. Just as Jesus was tempted to abandon the cross physically, we are vulnerable to the temptation to abandon mentally, spiritually, and/or emotionally. We may abandon the cross in our thinking when we define and direct our thoughts by human reasoning, means and ends, rather than by Biblical reasoning, means, and ends.

Paul, the Apostle, in Philippians 2 brings together the suffering of Jesus with the admonition that we possess the same mind that Jesus possessed.

Our danger is to be wooed by the thought processes of the world and to leave the thought processes of the Scriptures. We face the temptation to divorce the cross from everything but our "spiritual" lives. But such sectioning off of our lives is a human impossibility and spiritual schizophrenia is the natural result.

There is a danger that the cross be abandoned in our worship. Contemporary "worship centers" omit the cross physically so as not to offend "seekers." All this accomplishes is the offending of God. For a seeker after God, who will not reckon with the cross, will not find God—but some other spiritual reality costuming itself as God. God is approached only through the cross of Christ.

Elsewhere worship is so centered on our own needs, our own feelings, and our desire to "get more people in," that we reject the cross for more utilitarian "spiritual" practices. The cross, nonetheless, stands, calling us to "reckon" ourselves to be "dead indeed to sin." Time after time the apostolic writers call us back to the cross. Their clarion call is back to that Christian truth of the redemptive work of Christ accomplished on the cross. The salvation which was accomplished, completed and delivered to the human race two-thousand years ago, is waiting for our bowed knee, broken heart, and contrite spirit. Once done, we rise in newness of life – as believers in the Lordship of the Savior, Jesus the Christ.

This danger, this tendency does exist, however, that we take the easy route and circumvent the cross while still thinking that we are remaining faithful. Charles Wesley knew the temptation for the mind and heart to wander from its cruciform anchor when he penned the words"

I want a principle within,
of watchful, Godly, fear;
A sensibility of sin,
a pain to feel it near.

Help me the first approach to feel
of pride or wrong desire;
To catch the wandering of my will,
and quench the kindling fire.

From Thee that I no more may stray,
No more Thy goodness grieve,
Grant me a child-like faith, I pray,
A tender conscience give.

Quick as the focus of an eye, O God,
My conscience make!
Awake my soul when sin is nigh,
And keep it still awake.

Adornment, over-doing what might otherwise serve spirituality, is also an ever-present temptation. That which is itself the epitome of degradation, that which is profane and success, that which has been often retained by criminals and public offenders, has often been the center of Christian attention. Adornment for holy beauty degenerates into adornment for attraction. Rather than beautifying the cross, we fall into the temptation of decorating the cross. That which was raw, rough hewn wood is made into gold, silver, and platinum and inlaid with jewels of all type and color. The cross is worn on chains around necks of people who, actually, do not know what it even symbolizes. There was a hurtful and uncomfortable reality of the cross of the Gospels. We must be aware that we not embrace the symbol as contemporary adornment consumerism tempts us while at the same time denying the disciplines that come with cruciform living.

One pitiful example makes the point of the contemporary ignorance of what Christianity is about and how little it impacts Western culture today. A mother wishing to purchase a necklace with a cross for her graduating daughter, entered the jewelry store and approached the clerk with her request. The very young clerk replied, "You wish a silver chain with a sterling silver cross. Would you like that cross plain or would you like one with the little man on it?" When this occurs, decoration overtakes dedication. Ignorance proves lack of historical and cultural instruction.

Who is this "little man" anyway? What does he mean? What did he do and does he demand or desire anything of us? Or is it entirely possible that we have, as a culture sunk so low that we adorn and no longer adore the cross and as a result those outside the church see no cross bearing in our lives?

Many who know of the cross are apathetic toward it. I can remember as a freshman in college saying, and hearing said, "Apathy is rampant on campus, but who cares?" That was the flakiness of freshman following the 1960s. But to take a, "who cares?" attitude toward the cross of Christ is to miss the serious decisiveness called for in Christian discipleship. There can be no Christian growth, no maturing, no spiritual direction if the cross is apathetically approached or ignored. W. A. Studdert-Kennedy makes this point: "At Golgotha, men at least crucified Christ, they responded to him with passion and with strength!" Today in Western life, the worldview is less physically painful to the Savior and more spiritually grieving.

When Jesus came to Birmingham
they simply passed him by;
They never hurt a hair of him
They simply let him die.

For men had grown more tender
And they would not give him pain,
They only just passed down the street,
And left him in the rain.

Still Jesus cried, "Forgive them, for
they know not what they do,"
And still it rained that wintry night
that drenched him through and through.

The crowds went home and left the streets
without a soul to see,
And Jesus crouched against a wall
and cried for Calvary.

You see, we are called to a grace-enabled constancy of vigilance lest we are swallowed up by culture's diminution of the cross of Christ.

There is a very real sense also that the cross of Christ is a cross of permanent effects. When St. Matthew records that Jesus was challenged with the words, "Come down from the cross," there is consistent biblical and historical evidence that he did not respond to that command. He permanently affixed himself to that cross, for he assured us that, "No man takes my life from me, I give it of my own accord." The sheer perfect will of the God-man kept him affixed to that cross.

Such a form of death kills; kills completely; kills finally. People did not survive crucifixions, for if they did they met the same fate the next day! You hung until you were dead. Through this shines the unparalleled and unequalled light that shows us that Jesus endured. He endured the cross, opening up the reconciling work between a fallen creation and a heart-broken Father. The writer of Hebrews in chapter 12 verse 2 reminds that Jesus "endured the cross, despising the shame." He endured what the fallen human system did to him, and he despised the shame it brought on the human race [nakedness in the time of Jesus brought shame on the one who viewed another's nakedness]. So Jesus is the victim who endures and the victor who, in being made a victim, brings shame to his murderers.

Jesus, on the cross, permanently opened a way for God to know the human person, and for the human person to know God. "In the cross of Christ, we find the revelation of the hidden God. To know Christ is to know God in suffering. The hidden God is the crucified God....Christian faith must speak of no other God, because God's humanity is the only means of access to God's divinity" [Carl Braaten]. And this access is a perpetual and permanent access.

The cross of Christ is also permanent in its effects relative to the immeasurable dimensions of its provisions. Not only, as Scripture records, is this provision for, "whosoever will," to come and receive, it is also world-wide in its scope; trans-racial in its inclusion; and timeless in its availability. It is this immensity which drives John to write, "He is the propitiation for our sins, but not for ours only, but for the sins of the whole world."

There is nothing larger than the cross of Christ. Robert H. Benson aptly notes, "It has been sed that the cross is the symbol of absolutely endless expansion; it is never content. It points forever and ever to four indefinitely receding points." E. F. Ellis echoes this. "There is no comma after the cross; the cross is a continuous affair." What God has created limitless, let no one curtail!

The cross of Christ is a cross of practical application. Nothing in the history of humankind has been so utterly married to everyday life as the Cross of the Savior of the world. It is for those of high office and those of limited facilities; it reaches the most cultured and those most forsaken; in each case, in every instance, the cross makes practical changes in everyday life. Identifying with the cross of Christ is always conspicuous. A person does not go from the death of sin to the life of grace without someone noticing the change; the difference. The cross-identified person becomes conspicuous – not showy, but conspicuous. A person cannot exchange loyalties from oneself to Christ without something obvious occurring. The outworking of the implications of the cross will be manifest. This is not a call to works, but a manifestation of grace. The graced person cannot be overlooked. People see such a person; they know such a person; and they treat such a person as one who has been with Jesus. There is no one "crucified with Christ" who is not also at odds with all that is at odds with the cross.

The cross is applicable as well in providing our consistency. "Only by getting things right about Messiah and message [the cross]," writes Braaten, "can we begin to make sense [consistent sense] about mission and ministry." T. R. Milford in a series of university lectures in London writes, "How easily...a university becomes a place where everyone can believe what he likes—and to allow that is the death of thought." The cross will not allow us such an unproductive luxury, as the death of thinking. Milford continues, "the word of the cross spoke of one thing that had happened in history as the absolutely real by which everything else was to be judged." This has historical, contemporary, and practical meaning. And meaning gives us consistency; coherence; unity. And for this, God "makes no conditions," Milford concludes.

Many today are in a flurry of contemporary activity brought on by the rapid growth and development of modern technologies. Silence is no longer golden, as we sang in the 1960s, it is non-existent. To be without cell-phone or Blackberry is to be less-than-human. This leads to "loose ends and shady margins," according to Milford. To even think of living coherently is foolish to the masses, it seems. We have become excellent in our ability to build without developing our capacity for foundations. The cross is a foundation upon which all kinds of coherent and consistent structures can be erected. On a foundation a structure finds form, balance, beauty, and usefulness. And where these are consistently found, it will not take long to find that they are on a firm foundational footing.

In New York State from whence I hale, there is a need to dig "footers" for foundations, at least four feet deep which places them below the frost line where no thrusting will take place during the cold of winter. The cross is such a deep foundation, below the line where it can be shaken by lesser forces. Called to be truly human, in the image *and* likeness of God, the human can, on the foundation of the cross, become courageous and hope-filled in the midst of the vicissitudes of life. When great exploits are called for, those who know the cross, fear nothing of lesser harm. When Apostle Paul wrote, "I can do everything through Christ who gives me the strengthening ability," he was stating more than a mere platitude. He was affirming that through the cross, the believer can do mighty and meager things because the ability comes from the Lord Jesus Christ.

Canon J. B. Phillips who wrote the captivating little book *Your God is Too Small,* and also translated the New Testament into a wonderful modern translation, writes, "sometimes the bearing of the cross is very far from being a matter of static patient faithfulness. The call is to high adventure requiring vision, courage, and initiative and the willingness to bear any variety of suffering under the cross." The contemporariness of the cross allows it to be "borne," according to Phillips. He continues, "bearing the cross does not always mean refusing to compromise with evil nor making sacrifice nor refusing to take the easy path. Sometimes it simply means gay and patient endurance of physical suffering, the winning of an intimate battle by the patience of the cross....[There may be] the particular cross of being a lonely Christian."

These are the areas of life where the cross may become conspicuous, consistent, coherent, courageous and common. And all these may exist to the glory of the Christ of the cross.

The cross is also the cross of potential glory. Apostle Paul in Galatians 6:14 wrote, "may it never be that I should glory or boast in anything except the cross of our Lord Jesus Christ through whom the world has been crucified to me and I to the world." This declaration of loyalty and dependence comes from one who had only been loyal to his own interpretation of the Law and his dependence only on himself. What a conspicuous change!

Is it possible, that this cross of Christ, so like other crosses of its day, nonetheless continues through the ages being so immeasurably different than they? Has it a drawing power which evokes from would-be disciples that dedication which says with the poet, *"I will cling to the old rugged cross, 'til my trophies at last lay down?"*

Chapter Six

Humility: An Initial Approach to the Cross
Prayer: A Real *Telos* of the Cross

"It has been said that religion begins with wonder"
T. R. Milford

"On Golgotha, Jesus through the cross definitively confirmed that he was the 'sign of contradiction' foretold by Simeon."
Encyclical Letter *Redemptorist Matre 18:23*

"It was not the human race who placed their sins on your shoulders, making you a scapegoat, but it was you who had freely taken upon yourself our sins...."
Hans Urs von Balthasar

"The cross is an anomaly. It is inconsistent with what would naturally be expected. The cross destroys the wisdom of the wise and frustrates the intelligence of the intelligent. Yet it is perfectly in line with a God who has always been full of surprises."

John Fischer

"He humbled himself," writes Apostle Paul to the Philippian Christians. One can only humble him or her self – others may humiliate you, but they cannot humble you. "Humble yourself in the sight of the Lord, and he will lift you up." We often interpret this as humility being the automatic tonic which will cause us to be raised in total victory. Jesus humbled himself and God lifted him up on the hard wood of the cross. Humility begins the crucifixion process. The crucified person has given up personal ambition and plan; has relinquished desire for pomp and ceremony; and has turned over to the will of God both power and prestige. To hold to any of these is to erase all manner of humility from one's thinking. Actually, humility is always a potential, for to reach complete humility would be to be tempted toward pride. The cross bearing of the New Testament, however, calls for a crucifixion of all that militates again our humility. God does not humiliate us as slaves or servants, he invites us to humbleness of heart as friends. This Christ-likeness is found in our approach to others especially. How we treat others speaks of who we are both in their eyes and in God's. The graced life is not always engaged in graced living. Oh, yes, it is there in potential and providence, but it is often lacking in practice. This is in our control, under the power of our choice. This is not Pelagianism or Semi-Pelagianism, it is Biblical truth. Choice is a Christian concept. Archbishop William Temple declared, "Humility does not mean thinking less of yourself than of other people, nor does it mean having a low opinion of your own gifts.

It means freedom from thinking about yourself at all." Fixed on the cross with Christ ["I am crucified with Christ"], secured, as it were with the very nails that held him securely there, gives us a humility that nothing can match. Can we sing the contemporary choruses that claim "Without him, I would be nothing?" Do we really hear what we sing when we intone "Amazing grace, how sweet the sound, that saved a *wretch* like me?" or has this hymn become so overly familiar that we know and enjoy its music with little or no attention to its lyric? G. K. Chesterton reminds us that, "It is always the secure who are humble."

C.S. Lewis called pride 'the Great Sin'. He wrote, "According to Christian teachers, the essential vice, the utmost evil, is pride. Unchastity, anger, greed, drunkenness, and all that, are mere fleabites in comparison: it was through pride that the devil became the devil: pride leads to every other vice: it is the complete anti-God state of mind....it is pride which has been the chief cause of misery in every nation and every family since the world began." And St. Vincent de Paul wrote, 'If humble souls are contradicted, they remain calm; if they are calumniated, they suffer with patience; if they are little esteemed, neglected, or forgotten, they consider that their due; if they are weighed down with occupations, they perform them cheerfully.'

How then is the cross attained, through humility – it is its initiatory position.

The "end" or *telos,* the purpose of the cross, is prayer. Everything Jesus says on the cross is a prayer. "Father forgive them," is a prayer of absolution; "Today you will be with me in paradise," is an answered prayer, answered with promise and assurance; "Woman, here is you son," is a declarative prayer of comfort; "I am thirsty," is a prayer of need; "It is finished," is a prayer of declaration; and "Father, into your hands do I commend my spirit," is a final prayer of submission and surrender. The cross is the bridge from humility to prayer. Only the humble can pray; only those "crucified with Christ" can humble themselves. There is a tangling of these truths to such a point that they cannot be untangled. To draw one string of the weaving is to undo the weaving altogether. This is why some call the cross, "radical," it is not worn around the neck it is carried on the back. The person who is actually humble will prove an oddity in the world. Such a person does not in any way promote the self, but rather lives for the agenda of another. He or she does not announce their identification with Christ, it announces itself, and the only person who can understand the loneliness of humility and of cruciform prayer is often the person themselves. Watch how and who politics for position in the local church or the wider denominations, and elect them not. Humility is not a virtue of the political. You cannot be president and be humble – you simply cannot get there from here! Aloneness is the cost of humility, and the grief of prayer unanswered is the yoke of the true person of prayer. "Nevertheless, not my will, but yours be done," is not only the cry of Jesus the night before crucifixion, it is the not dissimilar cry of all crucified ones who identify willingly with the Christ of the cross. Jesus' cross reconciled God to humanity and humanity to God. His cross, humbly taken up by his person, will be heavy and burdensome and will lead most often down lonely paths, but he is there and that makes all the difference.

Chapter Seven
The Christ of the Cross

"There must be something of the cross in our minds before we can say with confidence, 'It seemed good to the Holy Spirit and to us.'"

J. B. Phillips

"For us, the one thing needful is for mankind to recover the Rule of Life as Christ taught it, and to follow it, at whatever sacrifice; for we are convinced that if the answer to our perplexities, the remedy for our sorrow and sinfulness, be not in him, then there is no remedy, no answer. 'Lord to whom shall we go? You alone have the words of eternal life?'"

James H. F. Peile

"God shows us a man who gave his life away to the extent of dying a natural disgrace without a penny in the bank or a friend to his name. In terms of man's wisdom, here was a Perfect Fool, and anybody who thinks he can follow him without making something

like the same kind of fool of himself is laboring under
not a cross but a delusion."

Frederick Buechner

The Apostle Paul thoroughly and intricately expresses the nature of his Christ and his relationship to the cross and the act of crucifixion in Colossians 1:13-27:

"He has rescued us from the power of darkness and transferred us into the kingdom of his beloved Son, in whom we have redemption, the forgiveness of sins. He is the image of the invisible God, the firstborn of all creation; for in him all things in heaven and on earth were created, things visible and invisible, whether thrones or dominions or rulers or powers—all things have been created through him and for him. He himself is before all things, and in him all things hold together. He is the head of the body, the church; he is the beginning, the firstborn from the dead, so that he might come to have first place in everything. For in him all the fullness of God was pleased to dwell, and through him God was pleased to reconcile to himself all things, whether on earth or in heaven, by making peace through the blood of his cross.

And you who were once estranged and hostile in mind, doing evil deeds, he has now reconciled in his fleshly body through death, so as to present you holy and blameless and irreproachable before him— provided that you continue securely established and steadfast in the faith, without shifting from the hope promised by the gospel that you heard, which has been proclaimed to every creature under heaven. I, Paul, became a servant of this gospel.

I am now rejoicing in my sufferings for your sake, and in my flesh I am completing what is lacking in Christ's afflictions for the sake of his body, that is, the church. I became its servant according to God's commission that was given to me for you, to make the word of God fully known, the mystery that has been hidden throughout the ages and generations but has now been revealed to his saints. To them God chose to make known how great among the Gentiles are the riches of the glory of this mystery, which is Christ in you, the hope of glory."

Paul refers to the death of Jesus in verses 20 and 22. These references are pivotal to understanding the person of Christ and the means whereby he comes to dwell in believers [verse 27] and present to them the "hope of glory." The crucified Christ is a Christ who may and must be known by persons. He cannot remain unknowable. Even missionaries tell us that when they arrive at hitherto unknown tribes, they find worship of an almighty god just as Paul did in the City of Athens in the first century. People are created to know God.

John R. W. Stott, rightly remarks, "The only authentic Jesus is the Jesus who died on the cross." There is no other Jesus; no Jesus of fundamentalistic literalism; no Jesus of demythologized liberalism; no Jesus of mental or social construct of the modern progressives. There is only the Jesus of the Second Temple period of Judaism, the Jesus of history, of whom the Gospels tell us all we need to know. And they are authentic, authoritative and reliable. Any attempt to construct a life of Jesus without doing it backward from his death is doomed to failure. The cross begins Jesus' life in both directions: backward in history infinitely and forward in eternal future.

God's ways and means are to take us to and through the cross just as this Christ was taken to and through the cross to resurrection. The Christ of God is necessarily the Christ of the cross. McCulloch writes, "... unless men believe in Christ, the Church is meaningless and futile, for it exists to bring men to faith in Christ and to strengthen the faith of those who already believe. The fewer men who believe in Christ, the less the Church is worth defending for its own sake. For that reason a Church busy defending itself and not the doctrines of the New Testament, suits the devil's purpose admirably." The evil one is pleased by a de-emphasis on the cross of Christ and the Christ of the cross. At the least, the enemy of our souls would have us postpone our dealings with the claims of and person of Jesus Christ, and would celebrate greatly if we were to treat the Cross with apathy and disinterest. That, of course, is one of the most successful tools of spiritual destruction: apathy and disinterest. Nonetheless, God continues to focus everything on the work of the Son, attempting continually and constantly to keep us fixed on the Cross so as to bring everything into cruciform focus.

In the Scripture quoted above, we encounter the Apostle Paul expounding the incomparable nature of Christ. He has no equal in his person; no equal in the execution of his task; and no equal in the exercise of cruciform power. He is Christ, the Son of the living God, "in whom, and only in whom,

77

we have redemption, the forgiveness of sins" [Colossians 1:14].

It is evident from Pauline writings that this Christ is the Christ of redemption who returns the human race to God. Redemption means "to buy back." Jesus pays the price, *to no one,* but *by his person.* We often claim as one tires him or her self out doing a task, "they paid the price." No one received anything, but they exhausted the self in the process they were completing. God demanded no payment; Satan demanded no payment; Jesus was the personal payment for the purchase of our race. There is a dynamic and infinite difference here. Satan is thus unmasked of his pseudo-ownership of the race of humanity, and God is saved from the wrong-headed theology that said he held over us a debt like some cosmic consumer who needed to be satisfied with a payment worthy of his lust for more.

The vocabulary employed by Paul is that which reflects the actual reuniting of the repentant with God the creator. He, Jesus, "has delivered" and "transferred us;" he has granted us "redemption, the forgiveness of our sins;" and he has "reconciled us." These are the acts of the cross through which Christ returns us to a relationship with God as if it had never been broken in the first place.

P. T. Forsyth claims, "You do not understand Christ until you understand his cross. Nor have you measured the moral world. Such a fact as Christ or His Atonement only exists as it is intelligible, as it becomes home to us with a moral meaning and a moral nature. It is only by understanding it that it becomes anything else than a martyrdom, that it becomes the saving act of God. It is only by understanding it that we escape from religion with our mind; from religion which is all mind; from pietism with its lack of critical judgment; and from rationalism with its lack of anything else."

The prophet, Isaiah, foreshadowed this cruciform salvation when he recorded, "he poured himself out to death...he, himself bore the sin of (the) many, and interceded for the transgressors" [Isaiah 53:12]. Christ's passion and crucifixion was *for* us, with the express purpose that he "intercede for transgressors," and return us to God. This is the Christ of the cross; this is the centrality of the Cross. Here the human need is recognized, understood, identified with, and redeemed.

John R. W. Stott writes, "the beneficial purpose of his death focuses down on our reconciliation." Leslie Weatherhead agrees, writing, "the words of Jesus about his suffering and death reveal that he willingly committed himself to some mighty task, costly to him beyond our imagining, but affecting for all men [sic] a deliverance beyond their own power to achieve, and that in dong so he knew himself to be utterly and completely one with the father." This was the will and purpose of God: humanity's reconciliation.

This is the Christ of the Cross. Paul is unequivocal in Colossians 1:22, "he has now reconciled you in his fleshly body through death (the cross)," thus inseparably relating our reconciliation with his crucifixion. It is impossible to have reconciliation without the Cross; it is impossible for the Cross to not effect reconciliation. He is the Christ of redemption who returns us to God.

Christ is also the Christ of interpretation, revealing God to us. He alone is, "the image of the invisible God" [verse 15]. "He who has seen me has seen the Father," declares Jesus in the Gospels. To hold out any hope of learning something of God apart from discovering it through Jesus, himself, is an exercise in futility; a possessing of illegitimate hopes; and the manifestation of Christological ignorance. Jesus is God incarnate. He knew in some great sense that he was God, and his followers grew in their knowledge of this, and many of his enemies, and his Enemy indeed, knew he was God. His cross is related to his incarnation as a revelatory enactment of the purpose toward which incarnation moved and to which the Cross was pointed. Again hear P. T. Forsyth: "It is sometimes said that the great question of the hour for the Church's belief is Christological; it is the question of Christ's person. That is true. But it is the question of the cross all the same. We know the Incarnation only as the foundation of the cross. It is from the base of His cross that the stair descends to it. For the question of the Christ is the question of the Savior."

Thus he interprets for us what God is like [verse 15]; he thus interprets everything else [verse 16]; and he declares that in Christ all things find their right and ability to exist [verse 17]. Apart from

80

Jesus, the human person cannot know these things.[5] John Stott continues: "The achievement of Christ's cross must be seen in terms of revelation as well as salvation. To borrow some current jargon, it was a 'revelatory' as well as a salvific event. For what God did there for the world he was also speaking to the world. Just as human beings disclose their character in their actions so God has showed himself to us in the death of his son."

So the Cross becomes a word as well as a way. Jesus is a revealer of the person and attributes of the Godhead and an interpreter of those things to the human race. All of this is in the context of the Cross of Calvary.

We are continually in our study of other works on the Cross, drawn back to its being a "work of Christ." In this sense, "the crucified Jesus is the only accurate portrait of God the world has ever seen" [Baker]. It is in the crucifixion that we see God's humility; his vulnerability; his love. C. S. Lewis paints this portrait: "God could, had he pleased, have been incarnate in a man of iron

---

[5] The scandal of the particular when it comes to Jesus as the only way to God, means the only way to the God of the Bible: the Hebrew/Christian God of the Old and New Testaments. Many other faiths have other gods if any. For example Buddhism is non-theistic in some of its manifestations. Not everyone who has faith wants or looks for what the Hebrew or Christian seeker seeks. We would call some things hell: reincarnation; nirvana; "oneness with the universe;" or "the loss of self in god." Christian teaching is none of these, and therefore, if one is looking to the God of the Hebrew/Christian Scriptures, we can affirm with assurance that Jesus is, "the way, the truth and the life. No man comes to the Father but through" him. We put no others down by lifting up Christ who said, "And I, if I be lifted up, will draw all men unto me."

nerves, the Stoic sort who lets no sigh escape him. Of his great humanity he chose to be incarnate in a man of delicate sensibilities who wept at the grave of Lazarus and sweated blood in Gethsemane. Otherwise, we should have missed the great lesson that it is by his will alone that man is good or bad and that feelings are not, in themselves, of any importance. We should also have missed the all-important help of knowing that he has faced all that the weakest of us face, has shared not only the strength of our nature but every weakness of it except sin. If he had been incarnate in a man of immense natural courage, that would have been for many of us almost the same as his not being incarnate at all."

What a magnificent reality this Christ Jesus, through cruciformity, reveals to us. The inseparability of the Cross from Christ and the Godhead is recognized and celebrated and held with no little gratitude. Oswald Chambers writes, "Most of the emphasis today is on what our Lord's death means to us: the thing that is of importance is that we understand what God means through the Cross!" And God means to reveal himself to us in this Cross, in such a way that we comprehend and subsequently *know*.

Christ of the Cross is the Christ of adoption who relates us to God. We are not only returned to a Creator, we are related to our Father [Colossians 1:18-20] This essential truth moves us from the creature-Creator existence to the child-parent relationship. It is a provision which no other faith

82

system provides or seeks to provide and it is an essential aspect of the concept and doctrine of salvation.

Again, in the words of Oswald Chambers: "There is nothing more certain in Time and Eternity than what Jesus did on the Cross: He switched the whole human race back into right relationship to God and made the basis of human life Redemptive, consequently any member of the human race can get in touch with God now." This is theologically known as "prevenient grace."

Relationship replaces alienation; family replaces individualism; belonging replaces detachment – all in the Cross of Christ. This is the intent of the Cross: to adopt us into the family of God and to make us, as it is written, "joint heirs" with Christ. You and I, therefore, become part of the "all things" which are reconciled to the Father.

Canon J. B. Phillips comments: "God's great act of reconciliation accomplished through Christ is of cosmic significance, and we should be rash to set any limit on its effect. As John pointed out, Christ 'is the propitiation for our sins and not for ours only, but for the sins of the whole world' [I John 2:2]. Yet when this tremendous act dawns significantly upon the individual heart and mind, the effect is intensely personal.... Millions since St. Paul's day have found forgiveness, freedom, and confidence in God in accepting personally a reconciliation that they themselves were powerless to make."

"Thus," writes John Stott, "reconciliation, peace with God, adoption into his family, and access into his presence, all bear witness to the same new relationship into which God has brought us." This is cruciform "shalom."

Then, too, we find this cruciform Christ to be the Christ of completion who confers on us God-likeness. There is no partial work accomplished by the Christ of the Cross. He never redeems one and leaves that one where he or she was spiritually or otherwise. When Christ begins a good work; when new birth is granted to the soul; when new thought patterns are given to the mind; and a new companionship given to the embodied soul [the self], then we begin to see the aim of the Christ of the cross –that is, to finish what he begins. The entire being is impacted by this Christ who has set the goal and made the gracious provision for the renewing and remaking of the entire person after the image of himself. The old desires, called, "fleshly," or "passions," are doomed for complete removal [Galatians 5:24].

In *Free to be Different,* Jeeves, Berry and Atkinson write, "What God has given us is not to be regarded as a static endowment. Our character can be refined. Our behavior can change. Our convictions can mature. Our gifts can be cultivated...We are indeed, free to be different!"

Though this work of completion is tedious – extremely difficult at times, and will take all our life long, it is nonetheless the process through which Christ carries us. J. Gregory Mantle, commenting on the word "reckoning" in Romans chapter six, explains something of this process when he writes,

"A great difficulty with many, is the maintenance of this reckoning, until the act of faith grows into a habit and sinful habits are replaced by those that are of the Spirit of God....[A] plant has condemned a leaf to decay, and the moment the silting-up process begins, the leaf is doomed. It may be weeks before it falls off, but it is as good as dead already. The plant never goes back on its resolve, if we may so put it, to deny that leaf further nourishment, and to throw its sap in another direction. Let us learn this lesson. Evil habits, which are the growth of years, are doomed the moment we put the cross of Christ between ourselves and them, and if we keep the cross there, never going back on the first reckoning, the fate of those sinful habits is irrevocably sealed, even though for weeks they may seek to regain their former ascendancy. We must keep on reckoning."

Paul, the Apostle, in Colossians 1:28 speaks of this completion as the goal of evangelism and nurture in the Church. This is Christ's goal; our end; our *telos*; god-like-ness reflecting and being shown through us.

The hymn writer put it this way,

Complete in Thee! no work of mine
May take, dear Lord, the place of Thine;
Thy blood hath pardon bought for me,
And I am now complete in Thee.

Yea, justified! O blessed thought!
And sanctified! Salvation wrought!

Thy blood hath pardon bought for me,
And glorified, I too, shall be!

Finally, we see the Christ of the cross is a Christ of opposition rearming us with a defeating message. This is no declaration of a victorious Christianity over everything else in the world, rather it is a loving Christianity committed to the defeat of everything that is anti-God and anti-Christ. In this sense the cross of this Christ is contrary, very often counterintuitive. This is no mere amalgamation of man's best attempts at answers, rather Biblical Christianity is the revelation of a loving God in his Christ, reconciling the world, the cosmos, the universe and all that ever lived, lives, or will live on it in the person of the crucified One. Carl Braaten wrote, "In the vastly accelerated progresses of our modern days it is nothing less than a tragedy if the Christian retires into his own pieties and refuses to give specifically Christian witness to the problems which bewilder modern man." The enemy of our souls hates the cross and its Christ. There is antagonism to the Christian message of love and of freedom; of rejoicing and forgiveness. But the Christian who understands the Christ of the cross is rearmed with an artillery aimed at softening the heart and winning the battles with evil by the sword of love. Braaten concludes, "The cross-bearing life arouses conflict and strife; Christian ought to expect that they will be regarded as sheep for the slaughter."

St. Aiden, one of the Celtic greats insightfully penned these most haunting and hopeful words, *"If you cannot cherish what it is the Lord is doing in your life, at least do not waste what he is doing in your life. Lay down the self-pity, and with all the strength and grace that he allows you, yield to his work. If you cannot make it up within you to yield totally to your Gethsemane (most of us can't) then at least yield up to the light the dark feelings of resentment and bitterness that are trying to hatch inside you.*

One day you are going to come to the conclusion that serving the Lord is mostly crying...and suffering...and agonizing. What can you do in that sad hour? Nothing really, except bend over double and absorb into your being those sufferings, sufferings which really belong to the church. In that hour, bear her sufferings for her. And if you happen to look up, you will see her going on her way, gloriously rejoicing. She will be oblivious to the fact that she is, at that moment, so very glorious because you have suffered."

The Christ of the Canon of Holy Scripture is the Christ who challenges; he changes the character of men and women without destroying their essential personality; he then bends and twists and lovingly molds them into his own image, the *imago dei* of Genesis 1:28. Anything less that this, misses the fullness of Biblical redemption, salvation, and reconciliation.

Chapter Eight
The Benefits of the Cross

"We go to Calvary to learn how we may be forgiven and to learn how to forgive others; to intercede on their behalf; to join the noble band of intercessors."

S. J. Reid

"The cross of Christ, on which he was extended, points, in the length of it, to heaven and earth, reconciling them together; and in the breadth of it, to former and following ages, as being equally salvation to both."

Samuel Rutherford

"In the cross, God descends to bear in his own heart the sins of the world. In Jesus, he atones at unimaginable cost to himself."

Woodrow A. Geier

"Through his death on the cross, Jesus Christ not only readjusts a man in conscience and heart to God, he does something grander, he imparts to him the power to do all God wants. He presents him with divinity, i.e. the Holy Spirit, so that he is garrisoned from within and enabled to live without blame before God."

Oswald Chambers

"Christ came for all people....He came to Bethlehem, certainly. He did come to that little land that lies between the seas. But this message does not have any geographical or astronomical meaning. It has nothing to do with kilometers and distances and continents and mountains and towns."

Aiden Wilson [A. W.] Tozer

"The Redeemer was God's gift....the value lies in the obedience, the holiness [of Christ]."

P. T. Forsyth

"The more the conscience is affected by Christ's words or behavior, writes P. T. Forsyth, the more is that standard generated within us which demands the atonement in the cross. It was the Christ of the latent cross that said these words and did these things." George Peters in his magnificent three volume work *The Theocratic Kingdom of our Lord Jesus Christ,* wrote paralleling this, that, "The benefits flowing from it [the cross] are now visibly presented and become more practically experienced until the world itself is embraced in their enjoyment. Following the Word, step by step, it will be found that the sacrifice [of the cross] forms an eternal basis for the kingdom itself."

The far reaching benefits of Christ's self-sacrifice [not to anyone, but by Someone] are not only historically verifiable and real, they are a present experience and in a very real sense a future promise and production of this "finished work" which Jesus, the Christ proclaims from the cross itself.

The benefits of the cross appear to increase in geometrical proportions as we move into the future away from the actual historical occurrence of the crucifixion. Nothing related to Jesus Christ ever diminishes, everything increases, yet, nonetheless, every provision is available every moment of history since Jesus proclaimed, "It is finished!"

This is one of the intrigues of the concept of heaven, or, rather, of the new heavens and the new earth. Far from being places of boredom, sameness, uniformity, they are rather the timeless, yet special provisions of the cross of Christ which will continue to expand and renew and unfold before the watching eyes and listening ears of the redeemed. Wonder is the virtue of seeing the unbounded and timeless within the framework of the immediate and the limited.

But lest we become too fanciful and heavenly minded, too theoretical and not earth-pertinent, it will be helpful to understand some simple biblical statements concerning the provisions of and benefits of the cross.

The Apostle Paul in I Corinthians 1:18 wrote, *"For the word of the cross is to those who are perishing, foolishness, but to us who are being saved it is the power of God."* The cross of Christ is the epitome and fount of all spiritual power. Spiritual power is not something we see break up from fountains deep within us, rather such power is seen in the influx of power from outside ourselves. Love and grace become overcoming powers, defeating the powers of self, of surroundings, of systems. Forsyth predicted the dislike of this thought. "Nothing is so resented by the natural self as the hearty admission of man's native lostness and helplessness especially when he thinks of all the heroisms, integrities, and charities which ennoble the [human] race. It is not always pride, it is often a mere natural self-affirmation." But the cross of Christ renders this self-affirmation powerless and replaces its impotence with the potency of cruciform enablement. Such a benefit is not the annihilation of the self; not the mortification of the affections; not the habitual trying to win that which is only obtainable and not attainable, rather it is the habitation of Holy Spirit in the heart of ones who own the cross of Christ – now graced, they are able to do all things in God's time, in God's way.

This power which is inherent in the cross of Christ, is practical power. It is power to know: to be and to do. The cross allows me to acknowledge myself; to recognize what I am in the presence of he who is; to see myself as God sees me; and to understand the position I am in: in need of a Savior. This power to know also informs that there is a Savior I may meet. I am not left alone with my sin and my guilt, I am a fit candidate for the saving work of Jesus Christ. P. T. Forsyth wrote, "God's controversy with man [sic] draws to a head in the unity of reconciliation, which solves the tragedy of guilt and grief." And this is no mere "spiritual" spirituality: this is a salvation available to individuals precisely because it is available to all individuals. It is a salvation that has shaken and turned upright the entire cosmos: the entire creation. We are invited to learn this and you and I *can* learn this because of the cross which is our power to comprehend.

Encountering the Savior leads me to know that there is a salvation to appropriate. "The way of the cross is the way of light," says a Medieval Latin proverb. To know with the knowledge of the cross is not only to have a personal salvation but to see with a light that before was shadowed. There is in this knowledge of the cross a power which we now own; a security which we can now experience. This is never found in the doctrine, a Creed, a confession, or some party of Christianity which thinks it is right at all costs. The cross gives the only knowledge which will set the mind at peace, the heart at rest, and the soul in security. It is only the light of this cross that can light a path and move one from the shadows to the light of God. These are inestimable benefits of the cross of Jesus Christ.

The cross of Christ also grants us the power to be. This is precisely what is being said by John in his gospel winning chapter 1 verse 12 we read, "but as many as appropriated him, he gave to them a legal right to become born -- one's of God, to those who place their trust in his name." It is by the power of the cross that we can appropriate the benefit of being a child of God. Through it we become able to become—by grace. It is as if there is no limit to the wonders of the benefits of the cross of Christ

Finally, the cross is the power to do. So often wrapped tightly in the doctrine of "justification by faith," believers fail to see that there is a necessary, parallel, and corollary action that follows the embrace of the cross. We are reminded once again that there is no Hebrew word in the Hebrew Bible for "faith." We only find words that relate to faithfulness. On the other hand clergy encounter believers running to and fro crying that it is impossible to live the Christian life. And they are right; but for the power of the cross. The answer comes from the cross itself. Provision has been made; purpose has been established; and power has been made available in grace for you to do what God wills you to do. As a matter of fact that is a close definition of great supply. The greatest daily benefit of the cross is that there is available to you and to me an enablement to do the truth; to accomplish the will of God; and to do the works of God. The "I can't," of the whimpering believer must be met with the "I will," of the confident saint. And though we will acknowledge that this is not easy and may be quite difficult the willingness may soon look back and see the accomplished.

When Jesus, in John 15:5, said, "apart from me you can do nothing," he was not saying that we would be idle. Rather he implies that if we want to be active our activity will find its dimensions and its dynamic in the very provision of the cross. As a unequipped and weak and unworthy as one may feel the cross gives the power to do anything which God wills that I do.

And thus we see the cross as the wisdom of God -- His will; his enablement; his glory. St. Paul in I Corinthians 1:24 echoes the truth that the cross is the wisdom of God. This is the light; this is the insight; this is the wisdom; and this is the knowing of the mind of God in an infinitesimal part, but a part nonetheless that shows us we have done well.

The wisdom of the cross is a wisdom and understanding which comprehends according to the logic of redemption. We believe in the supernatural; the miraculous; the mysterious; the marvelous interventions of God into the lives of individuals and into the life of his church. We can see beyond the

95

natural limitations of the physical world. This is a wisdom of the Holy Spirit over and against the wisdom of the flesh [I Corinthians 1:26]. Gradually we begin to see human strength as weakness and God's apparent weakness as strength. One writer said, "in God's plan the cross of Christ ceased to be an instrument of torture and changed and became the greatest glory." When our human mind says impossible, when we cannot agree with God's will, when naturally speaking all seems irredeemable, when situations appear hopeless we suddenly see God's hand at work in and through us. The cross is the wisdom of God which more often than not runs counter to manifest wisdom of the current culture and age. Such wisdom allows us to understand and accept the paradoxes of the nature of things whenever Christ is figured into a circumstance or situation. This is readily seen in a poem penned by Sen. Jeremiah Denton, written when he was imprisoned by the North Vietnamese. He wrote:

> *The soldiers stare, then drift away*
> *Young John finds nothing he can say.*
> *The veil is rent; the deed is done;*
> *And Mary holds her only son.*
>
> *His limbs grow stiff, the night grows cold,*
> *But naught can loose that mother's hold.*
> *Her gentle, anguished eyes seem blind.*
> *Who knows what thoughts run through her mind?*

Perhaps she thinks of last week's palms,
With cheering thousands off'ring alms,
Or dreams of Cana on that day
She nagged him till she got her way.

Her face shows grief but not despair,
Her head though bowed has faith to spare,
For even now she could suppose
His thorns might somehow yield a rose.

Her life with Him was full of signs
That God writes straight with crooked lines,
Dark clouds may hide the rising sun,
And all seem lost, when all be won!

This seems to capture the hopefulness of the seemingly hopeless. But it is truth in paradox we find in this poem.

The apostle Paul in one place tells the Corinthians believers that he is determined to know "nothing among them except Jesus Christ and him crucified." In no way would we even begin to think that this is easy to say or easy to do. But Paul, the cranky convert, seems to think that the power of the cross makes it able to be accomplished.

In the book of the Revelation we seem to be reminded that the ascended, enthroned Jesus Christ will continue to bear the evidence of his sufferings on the cross but now as a unique signal of his victory.

You and I benefit as his children. He is our intercessor; he is our mediator; he is our promised returning Lord; and all because of the provision of the cross. By this one man; through this one action; all of humanity becomes a beneficiary. The thought of this is beyond human comprehension. The reality of it is an essential part of divine revelation.

Chapter Nine
The Cross as Radical Wonder

"Christendom is an effort of the human race to go back to walking on all fours, to get rid of Christianity, to do it knavishly under the pretext that this is Christianity, claiming that it is Christianity perfected.

"The Christianity of Christendom...takes away from Christianity the offense, the paradox, etc., and instead of that introduces probability, the plainly comprehensible. That is, it transforms Christianity into something entirely different from what it is in the New Testament, yea, into exactly the opposite; and this is the Christianity of Christendom, of us men.

"In the Christianity of Christendom the Cross has become something like the child's hobby-horse and trumpet."

Soren Kierkegaard

"The cross, the death of our Lord upon the cross, is not something to be regretted. It is not something to be explained away. Nor is it something to be kept out of sight and hidden....So you do not regret the cross, and you do not try to forget it or idealize it, or philosophize about it, and turn it into something beautiful....No, what you say is this, 'I glory in it.'"

Martin Lloyd-Jones

"The cross allows us to encounter the greater reality of God, and shows up the inadequacy of human language and concepts to fully articulate that reality."

Alister McGrath

"The mystery shrouding the cross cannot be reduced to something we can completely understand as human beings. The truth of the cross is beyond and behind and before us, bigger than anything we can hold in our hands. Without the mystery, sacrifice turns into sentiment and substitutionary death into drama."

John Fischer

The Apostle Paul, in his first letter to the Corinthian Church deals explicitly with the wonder and majesty and awe of the cross of Christ. In First Corinthians chapter one we are told that there *is* such a thing as "the word of the cross," which is none other than the testimony and affirmation of the actions, the historicity and reality of the cross in time and space—hardly enough to inspire awe in anyone – men spread eagle on a wooden cross on the garbage dump of Jerusalem – awe? But give this despicable reality a proclamation; make of it an action which produces that which the church has proclaimed for millennia, and you get two possible reactions: "it is foolishness' [I Corinthians 1:18]; a stumblingblock [I Corinthians 1:23]; or it is interpreted through its mystery as "the power of God" and the "wisdom of God" [I Corinthians 18, 24]. You see, it is the lens through which you view the history: either it is merely a brigand receiving his just reward, or it is the Savior of the world. The two interpretations have held parallel sway for over two millennia.

But for those who will to see, it is just here where the wonder strikes the thinking mind the most: that something so onerous, so distasteful, so uncivilized [as the Jews considered crucifixion – and the Romans-at-large] would become so very religious, so uniquely spiritual, so indescribably central to what would become the greatest religion in the world in terms of numbers into the 20th century. And how could a rude cross in 33AD have anything divisive about its existence for the sake of God?

Yet nothing in history has so divided the opinions and convictions of the human race as has the person of Jesus Christ as known through his crucifixion, which, for all intents and purposes runs cross-currents with all the world sees and values as powers. All Jesus' followers proclaim him as: "King of kings, and Lord of lords!" There is no other power. No event in the history of the human race has so dominated the horizon of human history, heritage, and hope. Steinke rightly notes: "God is a God who works through contrarieties," and it is this God who works through his Christ and his cross though his truth and message runs so contrary to the ways of humankind.

The wonder of the cross is found in its pertinence. John R. W. Stott lecturing at Alliance Theological Seminary in Nyack, New York, noted that the human person has three needs or inner longings. They may be conscious or unconscious. First there is the need to know transcendence; second there is the need for significance; and finally there is the human need for community. The wonder of the cross and the community which it produces meets totally these needs of the human heart and thus are inarguably pertinent to a faith tradition.

It is a great note to see that the cross gives meaning to the seeker. Though not an academic discipline to master; not a victory to earn; not some plateau to reach; not some knowledge to obtain; the cross is first and foremost the symbol of a metaphor

102

for a person to claim. Any propositional truth that one possesses as a result of encountering the cross is subordinate to knowing the person who hung on that cross. The reason the cross can provide the foundation of all Christians thinking and life; the reason the cross can provide a point of view or perspective on knowledge; and the reason the cross can be the foundation of Christian theology is because it bore the Christ of God. It is clear that before the cross is any thing it is a pointer, and it points to the person of Jesus of Nazareth. In this, the cross finds its meaning. It is no mere subjectivity; there is no meaningless action here; there are no trivial pursuits here. This cross gives meaning where only meaninglessness has reigned.

When the apostle Paul declares the cross of Christ as power and wisdom he is declaring a revealed mystery and the mystery is only known by those who believe in mysteries. That is why elsewhere Paul would tell us that the natural man receives not the things of God. For things that are simply and purely natural do not accept the reality of mystery. The cross then reorients the human person allowing a vision of God through the lens of mystery.

As this historic means of death took on a more and more symbolic and metaphorical meaning throughout the centuries it more and more became germane to use the name Jesus Christ and the word cross interchangeably. So when one spoke about Jesus Christ they were speaking of the Christ of the cross. And when they were speaking of the cross they were not speaking of the cross beams but of the one who hung on the cross beams. It is this interconnectivity that allows Paul to say the cross is wisdom for the fool; the way for the fearful; and the walk for the faithful. In this the cross manifests its awe. In this the cross betrays its Christocentricity. In this the cross draws all to itself: all creation; all humanity; all thought. There is nothing that is so bad that it is not drawn to the cross. If there was, the cross would not then be the center of reality.

One writer speaks of the cross testing everything. He is right. We must remember that just before going to the cross, Jesus said plainly, "Now is the judgment of this world." There is something real; finished; and currently applicable about this statement. The world is both judged and redeemed in the same act. This is awesome indeed. The cross indemnifies us from needing the world's ways to accomplish God's will. Power is met indubitably with the disarming immensity of love; the world's accolades are met with the humility of Spirit only enabled by the Cross; attainment is met with obtainment; glory is met with grace; and foolishness is met with a wisdom which defies human fathoming. And none of this compares with "the glory yet to be revealed." God's last word on the Cross, in the Christ, though complete has yet to have its glorious hearing.

So the cross becomes this center of Christian, even cosmic hope. In this action, Jesus of Nazareth, the Christ of God, marries the two theoretical metaphors which have *always been contrasted,* and finds a coalescing of contrarieties that can be discovered nowhere else. There has, for time immemorial, been the contrasting of the theology of glory with the theology of the cross. I believe, in the Cross, they meet in a theology of grace. The lists which contrast the theology of glory with the theology of the cross are available, and I won't waste my reader's time in reproducing them here. What is essential is that we see them each as what they are: propositional statements endeavoring to explain a non-propositional event. If the mystery is removed Christ does not become the glorious victor who is Lord over all creation. Rather God is left to become the Hallmark warm, fuzzy, submissive wimp who accepts anything humans proclaim in the name of God.

Right in the middle of all this is God: the God of grace. He is both the God of glory and the God of humility. Such a God is the God who is victor because he was first the victim. The reality of this cannot be grasped through mere propositional revelation. We begin with the propositional; the creedal; the confessional [in some cases] but we climb the stairs to get a bird's eye view of the entire landscape of the Cross and its effects and we see in Technicolor the indescribable panorama of what the Christus Victor [the "Cross"] has delivered to the cosmos. Try putting that into your proposition and see what happens.

Is it any wonder, therefore, that people, when speaking, let's say of the Holy Eucharist, make mention of "the Real Presence?" There is no other way to refer to the Eucharist without defining it, and in defining it we remove the mystery and merely have soggy crackers and insufficient wine with which to rinse it down. The cross not only gives meaning and transcendence to the seeker and awesomeness to the brain weary and earth-bound, it gives a journey to those without destination. The Cross is both a destination and a journey; again a coalescing of contrarieties. Paul, who carried impressive credentials in both Jewish and Roman value systems, counts them but dung to know the cross and the Christ who was thereupon crucified.

The cross brought eternity into time; another realm into the realm of the senses; an eternal Son as a little child. Everything the human person needs had been delivered, not in the wood of the cross, but in the Christ of that cross. Its wonder is its infinite giving and its illimitable inviting.

Henry W. Clark wrote so compellingly of the grace of that cross in its bringing of the other into the human experience. He said, *"The cross makes an entirely unique mark in the process of the ages, altogether unclassified under any of the terms that suffice to cover the rest of history's content...the sacrifice of Jesus has a quality possessed by no other....*

"In some wholly unique fashion, the cross was the touch of God's mind and God's hand upon a moral and spiritual history of the world.

"Whatever, in the atonement, happened within the world, happened only because something

happened - previously or simultaneously, or both, **beyond** *the world."*

Paul's credentials now got him nowhere and all of our attainments are but useless effort separated from that which is obtained in the all sufficient cross.

Here is where those things we wish to wonder about find their source. There is no pot of gold at the end of the rainbow, there is a God at its beginning. The awesome wonder is that we are delivered through captivity; given new life through death; and we find wisdom in the simple things of the world. The perceptions are inverted; the truth revealed; and the invitation extended. Those who speak of a "limited atonement" may just as well speak of some other silly thing which makes no logical sense. One cannot limit the atonement; one cannot limit the limitless One.

Make me a captive, Lord, and then I shall be free.
Force me to render up my sword, and I shall conqueror be.
I sink in life's alarms when by myself I stand;
Imprison me within Thine arms, and strong shall be my hand.

My heart is weak and poor until its master finds;
It has no spring of action sure, it varies with the wind.
It cannot freely move till Thou has wrought its chain;
Enslave it with Thy matchless love, and deathless it shall reign.

My power is faint and low till I have learned to serve;
It lacks the needed fire to glow, it lacks the breeze to nerve.
It cannot drive the world until itself be driven;
Its flag can only be unfurled when Thou shalt breathe from
heaven.

My will is not my own till Thou hast made it Thine;
If it would reach a monarch's throne, it must its crown resign.
It only stands unbent amid the clashing strife,
When on Thy bosom it has leant, and found in Thee its life.

Finally, it is essential to see that the wonder of the cross extends to the entirety of reality. Richard Rohr rightly observes, *"A Christian is someone who is animated by the Spirit of Christ, a person in whom the Spirit of Christ can work. That doesn't always mean that you consciously know what you are doing.*

"As it states in Matthew 25, 'When have we seen you hungry? When have we seen you thirsty?' We may have no idea that we do what we do for Christ. But Christ said, 'Because you did it, you did it for me.'

"It never depends upon whether we say the right words, but whether we live the right reality."

The right reality is the awesomeness which the Cross reveals and magnifies to the human person. We do not grow into grace, we grow in grace; we do know grow into knowledge, we grow in knowledge; we never become a member of the body of Christ for in Christ we are made a member.

These are a few of the infinite wonders of the cross. The cross and its Christ are unique; immutable; available; practical; relevant. In the parlance of the 21st century, such wonder is a "free download."

There's the wonder of sunset at evening,
The wonder as sunrise I see;
But the wonder of wonders that thrills my soul
Os the wonder that God loves me.
O, the wonder of it all! The wonder of it all!
Just to think that God loves me.
O, the wonder of it all! The wonder of it all!
Just to think that God loves me.

There's the wonder of springtime and harvest,
The sky, the stars, the sun;
But the wonder of wonders that thrills my soul
Is a wonder that's only begun.
O, the wonder of it all! The wonder of it all!
Just to think that God loves me.
O, the wonder of it all! The wonder of it all!
Just to think that God loves me.

The cross is by far, a superlative wonder...meaning that ultimately we cannot do it justice by mere human words and mere human concepts. It transcends them. And this begins with the idea that the cross is an objective reality. How in the world can a means of death become a symbol for life everlasting; life eternal? One cannot adequately explain this.

The writer of *Philosophy: The Handmaid of Religion* wrote, *"We fall far short of our duty as Christian preachers if we fail to confront the hysterics of the hour with the documented realization that the message we preach is rooted and grounded in a set of facts that are as nearly tested and verified as the relativities and contingencies of history permit."* This doesn't merely mean we are preaching objective truth, but it means there must be some substance, some superlative wonder that takes such an historical event and makes it as alive on Good Friday this year as it was in 33AD.

Chapter Ten
Cruciformity

"To repel one's cross is to make it heavier."
Henri Frederic Amiel

"Not he who scorns the Savior's yoke; should wear his cross upon his heart!"
Johann Christoph Friedrich von Schiller

"In an olive grove, the Father and his Son had agreed on the final issues of deliverance for this planet earth."
Calvin Miller

"Christ has redeemed us from a vain manner of living."
R. Neumann

The apostle Paul is forceful in his declaration of loyalty and goals. There is, in the reading of his epistles, no questionable area when it comes to the purpose for which he lives, or any word by which he is directed. Such is the case in his letter to the Philippian Church.

In Philippians 3:10 he clearly states his mental intent as an example for fellow believers to follow. He writes, "that I may know him, and the power of his resurrection and the fellowship of his sufferings, being conformed to this death." There is clarity in the apostle's statement. Knowing the power of the living Christ, and experiencing the union of personality with personality is an identifiable suffering with the Master. This would only be possible as he, Paul, was conformed to Christ's death. And, of course, that death is the death of the cross.

Conformity is a metaphor for molding, being changed, being clay in the potter's hands. It involves the experience of a reshaping, a total renewal, of one's previous attitudes and actions. The cross necessarily impacts one's total being - it changes him – that is its intent.

A. W. Tozer rightly said that a crucified man is characterized by three things: he is facing only one direction; he has no further plans of his own; and he has made up his mind that he is never going back.

There is, in realizing one is crucified with Christ, a deep consciousness that there is "no trespass of personality," on the one hand, but there is a new creation of Christian character on the other. Jesus' purpose in redemption was to execute the plan of the father as recorded by Paul in Romans 8:29. Those God foreknew he predestined to be conformed to the image of his son. This experience, this conforming process, is what is meant by being remolded in the form of Christ's cross.

There are two parallel truths which speak to the Christian regarding this reshaping process. First it is a partnership in Christ-like suffering. It is important to note that Jesus began suffering long before the Calvary experience. There was a very obvious and extended rejection of his person, repudiation of his purpose, and ignoring of his plan. The wise of the earth questioned his motives; quenched his message; and quashed his morals. You see, being remolded is foreign to the human heart's own purpose.

As persons being made cruciform in our lives, we parallel the Lord himself.

Jesus, in his cryptic messages and parables laid strong emphasis on the corporate nature of the Christian church and at the same time emphasized the individual nature of the will to follow. Contemporary believers who stress the individual or communal nature of Christianity will often come into conflict on one side of the continuum or the other. Many see individual Christianity as subjective and therefore "unreal," and other view the communal nature of the Christian faith and demean it as a radical and historical failure. Each, of course, is wrong at the very point of their criticism. If either understood Christianity *from the inside,* they would understand the two natures of the faith and that they are, of necessity, imperfect! The age old insult that we "use religion as a crutch," should always be encountered with, "but look who's limping!" "Faithing" as the literal Hebrew Scripture word should be translated, is a cause for insult from those who see no need to faith. Modern science did away with such Medieval superstitions, and modernity won from the beginning of the Renaissance until 1989 when the Berlin Wall came down announcing that the humanist experience, detached from a transcendent God is nothing more than a well decorated *cul de sac.* The "molding" work of God on the human life can begin when the scientific definition is owned and acknowledged, and recognized as inadequate in and of itself. The intellect, will, emotions, and spirit are stretched and formed and molded and processed by God when we move in the God reality.

In the molding and shaping of the human person to the cruciformity of Christ, we become less and less ourselves; more and more like Christ; and therefore more and more ourselves. So this molding and making is in the Christian's sufferings and in the Christian's death. "Die, before you die," said C. S. Lewis, "You will have no chance thereafter!" Death/resurrection metaphors are used to inform us of the direction in which God takes those who are his.

This is not inherently inviting, as many a mystic will tell you! Those who live into this are those who know that the Christianity of the cross is not an easy road to walk (ask our Lord, himself). And at this point, no matter how varied the believers' journeys may be, they all intersect at the cross when we face what Paul writes, "You are dead and your life is hid with Christ in God." We are invited by the cross, we suffer because of the cross, we die on the cross, and we are made by the cross. And though there is no question at all of the fact that God in Christ loves each of us as we are, there is little or no intention on God's part to leave us where we were found. "Behold, in Christ, all things (and persons) are made new!"

Christian believers, as are all persons, are members of a new order. Believers see and know this, though often they run from it because it is cruciform. Even churches for centuries have been built with a "crossing," a cruciform floor plan, to remind us, that as we approach the Eucharistic meal, we must pass through the cross. Belonging to God is belonging to one's maker – he who makes, molds best.

Chapter Eleven
The Contrary Cross

"There is only one ground upon which the Christian faith is to be preached, and that is the ground of truth. And so to preach it is to fling down a challenge. This is true: take it or leave it, as you will. This is the truth about God and about man [sic], revealed in Christ. This blows back to Hell where it belongs, the mistaken belief that life can be a bed of roses, or that a bed of roses has all the elements of a full life, and its demands that make us take life as it is, joy and sorrow, pain and passion, failure and success, and create it in fellow-workmanship and fellow-suffering with God and men [sic]. When it speaks of following Christ by taking up the Cross, it means that the truth must be established at all costs, that the good must be achieved whatever the pain in achieving it and that beauty must be found and known in life, no matter how fantastic seems the price of finding and knowing and revealing it."

Joseph McCulloch

"You cannot expect a believer to operate with one set of beliefs in his study and another when he is worshipping."

Alister McGrath

"His (Christ's) teaching is strangely at variance with the accepted standards and ways of life which we find in modern civilizations, and indeed in any civilization since the world first officially patronized Christianity...."

James. H. F. Peile, MA

If you have never once been put off by the contrariness of the cross as you read of it in Scripture, I wonder why that is? The Apostle Paul, who once, as Saul, was a radical persecutor of Christians, is, after encountering the Christ of a contrary cross, radically changed. There is little other than a residual wrestling with his pride that carried over from who he once was. The old became new; the one perspective was destroyed because real reality was now viewed; the one who was actively limiting truth to a sect in the world, was now opening truth to the world once cut off in his thinking and belief. Thus, the cross had an off-putting nature to it; a contrariness; a "negative" feeling initially. This was seen in the two works I referenced at the beginning of this collection: *The Reproach of the Gospel* and *The Faith that Must Offend.*

The very nature of our person encounters the contrary nature of the cross in our need to own our redemption in Christ. Often called conversion, this is not a mere changing of directions in life, but rather a radical changing of everything in life. Not only do we have character flaws; not only are there mistakes to be corrected; there are souls that need to be made alive! And this has been provided for all in the cross of Christ. The dam which keeps the flow of salvation blessing from flowing is controlled by the will of each woman and man. A, "Yes!" to God, is a "Yes, to a God who has already said, "Yes," to us in Christ. And so the contrary cross says don't remain in that dead state – come alive – as the dry bones did in Ezekiel's day when filled with the breath-giving Spirit of God.

The cross is contrary because modern psychology (and there is much good in it) has either determined everything I do I have no choice in the matter; or that everything I do, especially what is socially considered "wrong" is either someone else's fault or the fault of society writ large. The contrary cross says, "No!" to this. And hearing this "No," through "ears that hear" with more than mere wave vibrations, is a "No," that is invitational and not determinative and certainly not a final pronouncement. One old-time Anglican, preaching with evangelical fervor said, "The bad news comes first, and then never comes again!" The cross is contrary to hardness of heart: it softens persons. It is contrary to lethargy and laziness and moves one out of such complacency to activity and trust. It changes us. James Peile writes, "We expect faith to move mountains and to change the face of the world when we will not allow it to change the least of our habits and opinions." Ouch....So in this sense, the cross is a critical instrument: examining, judging, correcting, and using those who will allow themselves to be related to it in Christ. God has acted – an invitation has been given – complete provision has been made – come. "The cross reminds the Christian church that there is simply no room for complacency, self-confidence or triumphalism within its bounds," writes Alister McGrath.

This contrary cross gives deliverance from the need to be right; the compulsion to correct others;

and the vain need felt deeply by some people that they are God-ordained to run his church. The cross erases these things from the mind: new motives are given; new means are provided; and new ends or goals are prescribed.

Whereas Renaissance, scientific modernism, and godless humanism removed God from the throne of the universe and thrust humankind there instead, the cross calls, "Come down from the throne...the steps lead through the cross...and come out resurrected on the other end...no more throne...no more rule...no more power....Peace now reigns. This is scandalous to the modernist but it rings somewhat true or possible to the post modernist who has been disillusioned by the dead-ends of modernity. Could it be that to go ahead in the history of the world, we need to take a jump backward two-thousand years to a simpler faith and a peaceful Savior? More Christians are killing Christians as I write this chapter than ever before in history. The martyrdom of Christians is almost at its highest point in history. Should we not again raise the cross and allow it to usher in a peace which passes all understanding? Again, McGrath writes, *"The growing desire on the part of Christian apologists to accommodate their faith to the aesthetic and more presuppositions of their contemporaries inevitably meant that the sheer scandal of the cross became diminished. To use Goethe's famous illustration, the cross became 'wreathed with roses' – cultural sensitivity, romanticism, and sentimentality combined to change the harshness of the cross into a symbol of gentleness.*

The scandal and folly of the cross were set aside, as layers of accumulated tradition surrounded that cross with interpretations which it had never before possessed, allowing Christianity to clothe itself in more splendid garments than the rags in which it was born."

The condition of the post-modern world, not just Western culture, but the entire world, calls us back to the rags of our founding, and to the swaddling clothes which make a man a King.

Chapter Twelve
The Cross and the Church

"The church is on the cross; it is a martyr church, at the hands of the [sold out] Jewish leaders and [surreptitious] Roman elite; and then later by the Gentile [world]; it must win its throne as the Lord won his.   But the cross of the church is nothing compared with the cross of the world; though the world is already nailed to it, there is worse to come."

H. L. Goudge

"If I [we] am to be delivered, God must throw aside his dignity and dive into the unpredictable surf of sin and human suffering."

Calvin Miller

"Jesus is suspended between heaven and earth, repudiated by men and forsaken by his Father, thus restoring the unity between them.   Extending his arms he reaches out to both the sinner who goes back to him and to the one who turns away from him and yet could not hinder Christ to reach out to him.   The

vertical beam of the cross bridges the gap between God and man, while the horizontal one embraces the ends of the earth. The Fathers of the church therefore could aptly say that the cross had the dimensions of the whole creation; it is the dimensions of the whole history of the human race because it is in these three long hours of Christ's agony, the sins of all – from the first person to the very last – have been gathered and remitted. From now on the way to heaven is open to all: this is the teaching of the church."

Hans Urs von Balthasar

I have not touched on the theme of the cross and the church in the first edition of this book of edited homilies, but due to the condition of the overall church of Jesus Christ in postmodern Western culture, it is incumbent that something be said to bring the church itself, and not just its individual members back to cruciformity. We used to walk through the crossing when we approach the altar for the Holy Sacrament of The Eucharist. And today, many churches have moved the altar into the crossing. Either is a good lesson: the church is on the cross with its Christ before it is on the throne with its risen and ascended Lord. Since the Church is the manifest Body of Christ subsequent to the Ascension, it must needs bear the marks of that body: marks of suffering; marks of torture; marks of love; marks of resurrection and life. One wonders when the church of the twenty-first century is examined if there is any parallel between the church and the cross which founded and defines it.

There is no such thing, nor has there ever been such a thing as a Christian nation. This is not in the eternal scheme of things. The best we can get is a Christian church and it is important that we not be settled one little bit until we have allowed Holy Spirit to flush us through and through with the living water of the Word of God and made us as pure as redeemed sinners can be made this side of the grave. "Any church that thinks it stands, must take heed lest it falls," is a paraphrase of the Scriptures themselves. Churches too soon become systems. If something works one place we duplicate it somewhere else and soon we have clones instead of churches. It is the cross that embraces the human race and therefore forms the foundation of the church which embraces the entire human race. If any are denied membership, those that deny it are not of the church of Jesus Christ.

The author was once dismissed from a position because he allowed African-American adults and children to begin attending a "white-flight" church in the elite suburbs of a southern city. He wears it as a badge of honor, for that church, twenty-five years later is small, ingrown, parochial, and God's absence is evident. When God writes, "Ichabod" over the lentil of the door of a church building, there is no redeeming that which has willfully been surrendered. Remember, C. S. Lewis tells us that the door to hell is locked from the inside, and many churches have locked themselves outside of God by denying what the cross tells them to bear! We need not lock ourselves out because of race. It may be socio-economic levels; elitist attitudes [especially in many older Episcopal churches]; it may be dress; make-up; demeanor; facial hair; you name it. Whatever closes out another it is obvious it is not cruciformity which is the motive.

The broadness and comprehensiveness of the cross is what makes the cross central to the church. Pain and suffering are, by the cross, sanctified. That is why the Scriptures speak of "making up the sufferings of Christ." What begins with the head flows through the entire body. And it is as the body

126

feels the pain of its members and reacts with appropriate care and love that the church completes the work Christ gave it to do in the area of human pain and suffering.

The cross and the church find the world a suffering world, and it is through the suffering that it is redeemed. Not that suffering alone is redemptive, but rather that a suffering world, embraced by a suffering church, focused and sold out completely to a suffering Servant and Savior, redeems the world. It all necessarily flows from the cross. As with grace, all the benefits of the cross flow downhill.

The "patient" endurance of the sin, suffering, and pain of the world are felt by the church as the church "takes up its cross." This is very different and more completely intense than the individual-centered salvation of our culture. In this, I become less important, we become very important, and they, the world, become most important as the church takes a cross into the world. Such a world will be offended by it and find it foolishness. Such a world will more readily identify with it when it is presented in all its sanctified splendor and not in its diamond encrusted, far-removed, sanctuary-only use. An anonymous writer leaves us this challenge"

For all through life I see a cross,
Where sons of God yield up their breath;
There is no gain except by loss,
There is no life except by death;
There is no vision but by faith,

No glory, but in bearing shame,
No justice but in taking blame;
And that Eternal Passion saith
Be emptied of glory and right and name.

Chapter Thirteen
The Cross as Requirement

"The man [sic] who can be blessed is the man, who, like both the leper and the centurion [in Matthew chapter eight], is aware of the fact, and boldly prays for the exercise of the Lord's power."

H. L. Goudge

"When we are willing to consider the active will of God for our lives, we come immediately to a personal knowledge of the cross because the will of God is the place of blessed, painful, fruitful trouble."

A. W. Tozer

"The Son of God, unlike the mythical Atlas, bears the world upon his shoulders out of love, and is crushed to the ground under its heavy weight."

Hans Urs von Balthasar

Grace, however wonderfully embraced or however immensely understood does not erase the cost of grace. Bonhoeffer clearly keeps this truth before us. We dare not allow this concept to bring us to a salvation by works, but there is a very real Biblical sense in which grace produces what grace requires; grace enables what grace personifies in Christ.

And therefore the cross is a cross of personal experience. This will, of course, differ from believer to believer for no two experiences are identical, but there will be something of personal faith which grows from the baptismal covenant through confirmation and on to mature adult Christianity. When the questions are posed by the Bishop at one's confirmation, mature, experiential answers are given. This begins one's conscious discipline of the cross.

The cross is also a cross of moral imperative. There is no place in the crucified life for personal morality which takes no account of Biblical morality. Grace finds it anchor in the holiness of God and we are called to, enabled to, empowered to, and expected to act in holiness as God our Father acts. However imperfect our holiness may be, it is necessary for our Christian witness to have people know that they have been in the presence of genuine personal holiness and moral uprightness when they have been with believers.

In such an embracing of the cross as a moral imperative, there is a remaking of the self —

certainly not by us, but by the God to whom we bow. Many over the centuries have called it self-renunciation, and it may be that, but it is a self-renunciation that serves to bring us to complete and spiritually real self-fulfillment. In captivating our hearts he sets the real self free. Yielding up the prerogatives of self produces a reinvigorating of that which is so yielded and an empowering of the self which we thought we had given away. We are never more ourselves than when God makes us ourselves in the cross. So this moral imperative, in and through the cross becomes a moral indicative which glorifies our personal Lord and Savior, Jesus the Christ.

The discipline of the cross also brings to our attention the fact that the cross is a cross of faithful provision. What we do not deserve we receive; there is not cause-effect involved. Graced, we are graced. And often it is easier to give grace than to receive it. We are told by professional counselors that America is a nation "guilty of guilt." We are willing to confess everything except sin. But sin is the only reality which can be confessed. One demands the other. The most evidential thing one can say about the social ills of our world is that there is a reality of personal sins. If they are not the cause of the social ills, they are so very intertwined with the social ills, that without confession, forgiveness, and grace, there is no "healing of the nations," an exact Biblical phrase.

There are eternal and infinite possibilities for the spirit that is so surrendered and flooded with the benefits of the cross that the disciplines of the cross become natural and free.

Warren W. Wiersbe, the outstanding twentieth century Bible teacher aptly concludes, "To take up a cross does not mean to carry burdens or have problems. I once met a lady who told me her asthma was the cross she had to bear! To take up the cross means to identify with Christ in his rejection, shame, suffering, and death."

And before the Eschaton, the requirements of this life prove to us that life is not, "fair." Philip Yancey writes, "The cross exposed the world for what it is (prior to its deliverance); a breeding ground of violence and injustice. . . .Good Friday demolishes the instinctive belief that this life is supposed to be fair."

Chapter Fourteen
An Equal and Opposite Force

"Unless Christ is publicly exhibited as crucified—placarded before us week after week, in word and sacrament—we will, like the Galatians, drift toward the view that we begin with Christ and his Spirit and then end up striving for our own righteousness before God [Galatians 3:1-3]. Since even Christians remain simultaneously justified and sinful, we will always gravitate back toward ourselves."

Michael Horton

"Let us not attempt to fix the limits of the Lord's mercy; that it would be extended to all who in any degree could justly come under the blessed boon thereof ought to be a sufficing fact."

Source Unknown

The centripetal force is equaled with a corresponding centrifugal force which thrusts outward, away from the center. It may seem odd to include this, but it is the essential nature of the cross to open wide its embrace of the world. An Anglican collect for Good Friday captures this wonder as it says, "Lord Jesus Christ, you stretched your arms of love on the hard wood of the cross that we all might know your saving embrace. Help us to bring those who do not yet know you, to the knowledge and love of you; for the honor of your Name. Amen." The verticality and the horizontality of the cross makes God's great love diagonally embracive. No one falls outside of the reach of the All Loving God to reach and to save.

We too, as we are centered on the cross and its powerful centripetal nature are thrust equally outward into a world and a people who manifest great spiritual needs. Such a "sending out" is based upon Matthew 28:18, 19 as well as on multiple other texts. We are "thrust" into the world with a permanent security; with a Biblical mandate; for a Christ-glorifying purpose; and with the spiritual humility of Holy Spirit. Often seen as ambassadors for Christ, the believing church is a representative; a intercessor; an example; and a communicator of basic truths at a level of mutual understanding.

The centrifugal force of the cross is the sending out of the Crucified One's crucified ones. It is an assignment that can be raw and real as antagonistic antichrist forces in the world meet the believer who lives for Christ. The New Testament tells us there are three "enemies:" the world; the flesh (inordinate desires, not the material body), and the devil (the personalized evil one). As witnesses to Christ making us whole in the midst of brokenness, we will encounter those things that seek to break us: "the lust of the eye; the lust of the flesh; the pride of life." Many of these antagonists hang on for many years and attempt to thwart our witness, but Christ reminds us to, "be of good courage!"

Courage is a spiritual virtue applauded by the Lord, himself. John R. W. Stott captures this with the words, "Jesus, as much as pagan teachers, insists on courage as the primary virtue. The great difference between them is not the kind of courage they value, but in the motive to which they trace it. For Jesus, courage is not a matter of physical constitution, or for that part a purely moral quality, but the expression of faith in God. In the confidence that God is supporting them, men [sic] can meet all circumstances fearlessly, knowing they will overcome the world. Courage is thus a vital element not merely in the ethic of Jesus but in his religion." We might also strengthen this by saying it is a virtue in his kingdom. The kingdom of God calls for courage in that its weapons of warfare are utterly opposite in definition and use from the weapons of warfare of evil. Therefore, when the Christian is thrust into the world, he or she is thrust there with a mission which calls for courage; a purpose that calls for focus; and a Christ who calls for loyalty.

All of this centrifugal sending demands the centripetal anchor because we cannot be people who are always "flying off" in some unmoored way creating our ethics, our morality, our methodology as we go. McCulloch states, "We cannot revere the transitory, only the permanent." This cruciform message cuts across the atheistic naturalism of contemporary postmodernity; the materialistic scientific naturalism of the modern age; and the magical power-controlling pre-modern age. And during each era the Christian is sent *into* the age, the culture, the world, so to speak, with the message of the cross. It will offend some and many will find it foolish, but it is the only answer to the human dilemma of the day. The power we possess is a given power, and we are challenged with the purpose of God to proclaim, by incarnating his risen life, the message of reconciliation.

The Christian believer is, therefore, a "sent one." After calling us *to himself,* God sends us out in a very real sense, *as himself,* with the message that, "Christ is the propitiation (atonement) for our sins, and not for ours only but for the sins of the whole world."

The message is not the law, the message is grace. Every aspect of the message is saturated with grace and possesses the aura of peace (shalom). So instead of Sinai, we live and proclaim the Sermon on the Mount.

This, though an exposition of what the Kingdom will *finally look like* is also the model of what the coming Kingdom *looks like right now.* Each time we pray, "Thy Kingdom come, thy will be done; on earth, as it is in heaven..." we are requesting that the finality of the Kingdom sink down into the thin places of our lives where we can and must live the essence of what we will live always.

God chooses to show Christ to the world *through his people.* And the people of God, are always a cruciform people: anchored in the centripetal and thrust out in the centrifugal, and knowing the pain, stress, suffering, and anguish this can and does cause. God's people are a crucified people if we remember Paul's declaration, "I am crucified with Christ...." Oswald Chambers writes of the suffering of all when he writes: "Suffering is the heritage of the bad, the penitent, and the Son of God. Each one ends in the cross. The bad thief is crucified, the penitent thief is crucified, and the Son of God is crucified. By these signs we know the widespread heritage of suffering." What a dynamic Chambers captures here. What a suffering world needs is a suffering savior, manifested in its presence by crucified, suffering people.

The temporal world needs the suffering that manifests transcendence. The old magic of the church needs to be cast aside and not dignified at all and it needs to be replaced by the mystery of the sacramental life. That which is corporate in appearance must give way to that which is ecclesial in appearance. People want someone or something before whom they can legitimately bow. The sacramental definition of the church grants this answer to the deep, deep need.

The world is searching, not so much for answers as it is meaning. Everything from atheistic evolutionary scientism, to psychological reductionism or behaviorism, to philosophical nihilism, has convinced the human thinker that he or she is either a high class chimpanzee; a programmed and programmable machine; or a meaningless mass of well-formed matter. It is too late to give people a mere "how" to live their lives. The church preached all the "oughts," "shoulds," and "musts," that it could get away with. The church must now move from imperative proclamation to indicative living, for "the person who has a *why for living,* can endure almost any *how."*

Finally, after centuries of being told the greatest achievement of all is the individualism the human heart craved, we are finding that such individualism leads to loneliness, isolation, and purposelessness. So the human of the twenty-first century is looking once again for community. "I am master of my own fate," is not as true as once thought, for "it takes a village to raise a child." It takes a church to raise a Christian!

Recently when visiting my neurologist for an update on my Parkinson's Syndrome I told the attending nurse that I thought my neurologist was absolutely the best the discipline had to offer. She replied, "Oh yes, we raised her from a pup!" "We raised her..." that is why she is such a good doctor, she was raised by community and community is where humans thrive the best.

Into these needs, the cruciform believer is sent – not alone, but indwelt; not without a message – but with the cross; not to some unworthy race – but to the creatures who are made in the image of God. Could any work be more rewarding?

Chapter Fifteen
The Cross Casts its Shadow

"So we take our places in the midst of chaos, or pay homage to nonsense. If we let go of those instinctive inclinations to probe the chaos or grasp it, we may find ourselves in awe of it. And if we come before the cross in this wise, we may be chastened and know true wisdom. We may actually be strengthened to face in humility the overwhelming chaos and the numbing nonsense of our time...

"As we face the cross and the chaos, we may see that it is not God who is mocked in this crucifixion but we ourselves."

Sam A. Portaro, Jr.

"The Christian faith... will allow no slightest trace of sentimentalism and this, for us, is the very center of the cross. For we are, so we often say, incurably sentimental. We like to soften stark outlines and hang tinsel on naked wood. Leave us a little sentimentality; let us blur the truth about ourselves and about the realities of the world, and we will follow Christ. In all the terrible strength of Christ's love, there is nothing for us so terrible or so strong as his unrelenting truth."

Joseph McCulloch

There is a shadow to the cross of Christ. It is not a physical shadow which lay moving with time across a hill called Golgotha on a lone Friday we call, "good." Nor it is the shadow cast by the sun whose shining is gradually diminished as the Father forsakes his dying son. It is not a shadow cast by a central cross as an eclipsed eeriness spreads over the Judean hills, no it is not physical at all. It is not caused by the natural effects of physical light and actual barriers. It is not a shadow which can be measured for length and used for shelter from the heat. It is not a shadow on a hillside.

The shadow of the cross of Christ is a shadow on the landscape of eternality, and it is shed on the hillsides of the temporal and the eternal, and its shadow is one of blessing. One cannot encounter this shadow without knowing they have been with God. The light that causes the shadow is the "Lamb slain before the foundation of the world," as he hangs on the cross. It is only in the cross of Christ that the shadow therefore makes its darkening mark on all sides at the absolute same time. This is a shadow of uniform and ubiquitous blessing: the knowledge that one is conscious of God – conscious of God in whatever time, circumstance or place. The cruciform shadow is also a shadow of joy. Not happiness, mind you, but a shadow of joy, for it keeps one from the heat of the battle while one is in the very midst of spiritual battle. Joy is not the absence of melancholia, it is the realization that the cross is sufficient, in the midst of melancholia. This is no mere happiness; no giddiness; not a thing that causes unnatural smiling all the time. No it is blessedness and joy, not feelings of happiness.

The shadow cast by the cross is a shadow over the past – the tabernacle in the wilderness and the temple of Jerusalem – it is a shadow of the present when in approximately 33AD a man named Jesus from Nazareth hung on that cross-beam spread eagle for the entire world. It is a shadow for the future: for the days since the crucifixion and into our day and beyond. It is the will of the Father that the politics of humanity put to death his son – the powers win – for three days – so they think. The shadow of the cross lay over the gravestone which was rolled miraculously away from the door of the tomb, and allows doubt to be subsumed into the church's faith which carries us along even when we think all there is, is abandonment.

The cross also transforms human suffering. And though it may not be a well-reasoned answer, and though we may not "feel" the restructuring of reality, "the suffering of the present cannot be compared to the glories to follow." This is Scripture at its most encouraging. The cross's shadow lays refreshingly over all human suffering, redeeming it, and allowing God to take it up into himself, and for us to "make up" for that which was lacking in Christ's sufferings. [Do not ask me to exegete this completely – it is a statement one trusts or does not].

The writer of the book of Hebrews lists what he or she calls, "a great cloud of witnesses." These gathered saints are somehow surrounding those who are yet in the work of ministry, what the church used to call, "the church militant," for they understood that the church on earth was indeed doing battle with evil. These saints are cheering us onward. The cross is producing a shadow cast by those who have been "crucified with Christ," and are now somehow in a glory, a paradise awaiting the final and full resurrection of the body. It is a large picture as if you and I are in an Olympic stadium running a race and they are cheering us on, knowing somehow that through suffering, we will, nonetheless win. The victory of the cross is assured; assured even when, and particularly when we cannot see the victory – it must be claimed by faith – in hope of its reality.

Isaac Watts gave us this wonderful lyric to capture the wonder of this cruciform shadow:

Since I must fight, if I would gain,
Increase my courage, Lord;
I'll bear the toil, endure the pain,
Supported by thy Word.

There is no other shadow in which we can take our present and future refuge, but the shadow of the cross: not God's afterthought, but the natural outcome of a God gone Incarnate! And John Bowring exclaims:

In the cross of Christ I glory,
Towering o'er the wrecks of time.
All the light of sacred story
Gathers 'round his head sublime!

147

Chapter Sixteen
The Cross and 'Free Will' or
The Voluntariness of the Cross

"The cross of Christ is the point of reference for Christian faith; Christian faith is based upon it and judged by it – in short, the cross is the foundation and the criterion of Christian faith."

Alister McGrath

"The cross of Jesus Christ is as relevant today as it has ever been. It speaks to capitalists and communists alike, to all races, to every human being alive. Furthermore...it is not enough merely for us to listen. For the message of the cross changes lives and demands a response from all who hear it...It is God's message of hope for today—there is no other."

Christopher Catherwood

Infinite numbers of arguments over the centuries have been put forth on the issues of free-will according to foreknowledge versus predestination. [This author thinks he has it figured out, but it is for another time in another book...we'll see if I am willing for it to be written!]. The situation cannot "solve," because it is precisely the issue of endeavoring to fathom the mind of our God. Once we establish that such a thing is impossible, we remove ourselves from the hook and relax...at least we ought.

The cross in its objective reality is a call to choose him who, on the cross has chosen you. Karl Barth is not far off when de declares that in Christ all are elect because Christ is *the elect man!* Election, however, may not guarantee new life, since one is called time and time again to say an, "Amen!" to God's, "Come!" There really is "nothing to do but to come," according to Victorian lyricist and evangelist A. B. Simpson.

Jesus, himself, sought to be freed from this "cup," which he knew he would drink, for he says to the Father, "let this cup pass from me, nevertheless...." The "nevertheless," is the key word here. It is the word of Christian willingness for the will of God; it is the word of Christian submission to a picture which is larger than our "P.O.V." or point of view. In a postmodern age when "meta-narratives" are not supposed to exist, one encounters the cross which is completely a symbol of invitation, and finds in that invitation the basis of answers long sought.   All the answers are not there as on simplistic and sometimes dangerous bumper stickers like, "Jesus is the Answer."   No, questions remain, but in the cross, there is the fundamental essence of the grace and love of God wherein the answers we do find will be sufficient and the answers which continue to elude us are sufficient as well.   We remain satisfied seekers.

Jesus assured his followers that if he were to be "lifted up," he would "draw all people" to himself. This is the necessary fundamental understanding if we are to understand the other words of Jesus, "take up your cross and follow me." Our taking is because he took. We follow because he has gone on before. So in a sense this is voluntary, but in a real sense this is what we must do – we are compelled by the love of God to immerse ourselves in the flood of grace which finds its eternal spring in the work of Christ on the cross.

In the early 19th century there were stunning and solid Christian revivals of the Biblical kind in Wales.   William Rees, experiencing the renewing power of Holy Spirit during those days of revival wrote early on these words.   I cannot sing them without emotion for the cross is seen for its illimitable grace and wonder.   There is no human stopping, no human cessation to what God begins!

Here is love, vast as the ocean,
Loving-kindness as the flood,
When the Prince of Life, our Ransom,
Shed for us, His precious blood.

Who his love will not remember?
Who can cease to sing his praise?
He can never be forgotten,
Throughout heaven's eternal days.

But then follows the second and final stanza. Its powerful lyric is the summation of the extravagance of God calling for the will of the human heart and mind to decide in God's favor: he has decided in ours!

On the mount of crucifixion,
Fountains opened deep and wide;
Through the flood-gates of God's mercy
Flowed a vast and gracious tide.

Grace and love, like mighty rivers,
Poured incessant from above,
And heaven's peace and perfect justice
Kissed a guilty world in love.

Incessant grace and love call to all children, women, men, to respond and know that "heaven's peace and perfect justice" have done their work and the metaphor is that they have "kissed a guilty world in love."

Rankin proclaimed that," God loves enough to allow us to choose hell." But C. S. Lewis reminds us that the key to the lock of hell is found on the *inside!*" The implications are vast. The work of ministry; the discipleship of our mind and soul; the intimacy of worship of the Trinity; the immense fellowship of God's people all are ours for the taking. Our efforts are grace-based and grace-enabled, but they are grace-invited as God speaks incessantly to our wills. "Our wills are ours, we know not how; our wills are ours, to make them Thine," wrote the poet Tennyson. We cannot do better.

This is not romanticism parading as practical theology. This is essential theology being applied to the grit of human daily existence. It is not the insipid smile of the television "evangelist," who guarantees that "Jesus will make you happy, healthy, and feeling terrific!" This is the invitation to the will to be drawn through the realities of existence to the cross; to recognize that we have been "crucified with Christ;" and that the lives we now live we live by the faith of the Son of God who loved us and gave himself for us. Alister McGrath, an outstanding theologian of the Church of England convincingly writes: *"The theology of the cross recognizes the tensions of the Christian existence, exposing them for what they really are and allowing us a realistic sense of perspective into our situation."* This is the "working out" of one's own salvation with fear and trembling as Apostle Paul writes, for "it is he who is at work in you to will and to do of his good pleasure." God working *his pleasure* in you and me? I seldom feel that way...but *"I dare not trust the sweetest [frame of mind]; but wholly lean on Jesus' name!"* What is wrong with wanting to "be like Jesus?" Could the cross; could Holy Spirit; could God lead us in any other direction of character and life change and illimitable growth? The "no" answer is the right one, and it is why we pray for each other, and why we remember the deceased in prayer—that they go from "glory to glory" in everlasting life. Choose the cross, it will make all the difference.

Chapter Seventeen
The Cross and Eternal Glory

"Bishop Walpole, the father of Hugh Walpole, the novelist, once said to a friend who was weighing a life call: 'If you are uncertain of which of two paths to take, choose the one on which the shadow of the cross falls."

Rupert Hart-Davis in
High Walpole, A Biography

"Becoming a Christian means placing oneself within a community, and recognizing one symbol-the cross of Christ-as having been authorized and authenticated by the Christian tradition, from the time of the New Testament onwards. It is this symbol which exercises a normative and decisive influence over the Christian understanding of God and the world, and the Christian cannot choose any other symbol unless he is to compromise the integrity of the Christian tradition."

Alister McGrath

"It is not enough to know Christ as crucified and raised from the dead, unless you experience also, the fruit of this."

John Calvin

"Let us listen to the cross speaking in the form of exposition. There is nothing that so expounds the truth of God to us as the cross of Christ. The Bible expounds the same truth. The cross of Christ lays it open before us and makes it speak to us. Have you ever listened to the message of the cross? Have you ever regarded it as a sermon and sat and listened to it, and have you heard what it has to say to you? What an exposition of truth there is in the cross of Calvary's Hill!"

D. Martin Lloyd-Jones

"In the presence of the cross man dares not speculate about the degree of his goodness; rather he is at one cast down by his sin and overwhelmed by the joyous insight that God is the kinsman of the way!"

Johann Hieronymus Schroeder

"Till my trophies at last I put down; I will cling to the old rugged cross; and exchange it someday for a crown," has been sung by millions over decades in English and dozens of other languages. One would guess there may be theological issues with the phrases [there are in most hymns and gospel songs] but it is a devotional classic and I believe it is, precisely because it references the future glory of the new heavens and the new earth. Now I am not a "pie-in-the-sky-by-and-by-when-you-die" kind of fellow, but I am convinced through reading Apostle Paul on the resurrection; St. John in the Apocalypse; and Jesus through the Gospels, that there is to be a "Christic point" as Matthew Fox would call it or an "Omega point" as Teilhard de Chardin would name it, when the Triunity of God will be revealed to all creatures of all time and the new heavens and new earth will be created by divine fiat. Beyond that, I am a pan-eschatologist: it will all pan out in the end! [Apologies to serious theologians everywhere].

I must cast my lot with Robert Farrar Capon who sees the future as a blissful meal; a prodigal's party; a marriage feast. And the cross of history is the commitment of the present and the symbol of final completion. Remember, Apostle John tells us that he saw the "New Jerusalem" coming down from heaven to earth, and it was in Jerusalem where the cross was rooted on the garbage heap of Golgotha. This final work of Christ is complete; once for all; never to be repeated. When Jesus cried, "It is finished," either he meant finished or he did not. He

159

certainly didn't mean both. The fact of celestial redemption is complete; the benefits of cruciformity are available; and the promise of universal victory is sure. The glory of eternity is the essential finality of the cross. Resurrection will be the experience of every person who ever lived because our sacrifice, our representative went to the cross on his way to the tomb on his way to the right hand of the Father! Even the scholar N. T. Wright concludes his study of II Corinthians 5:21a and Romans 8:1 by writing, "Notice how the sterile old antithesis between 'representation' and 'substitution' is completely overcome. The Messiah is able to be the substitute *because* he is the representative." It makes it all about Jesus so that it becomes all about us. The prodigal son is welcomed by the totally forgiving father; the party is begun; the older brother is outside [with an invitation from his Father and a key to get inside] and he complains. Those who will not have the provisions of the cross, God acknowledges and says, "you don't have to have the provisions of the cross, but they are yours nonetheless." How do those theological tidbits fit the revealed Word of God? Calvinists begin to call me things that end with "heresy" when they read this. But that is fine. Calvin was only Augustine updated, and Augustine had much of it wrong – he did not write canonical Scripture. And if Augustine had it wrong, I may have it wrong, but I see an eternal excitement; and eternal glory; an eternal praise [where "every knee shall bow and every tongue confess that Jesus Christ is Lord to the glory

160

of God the Father"] to be far more in keeping with the parables of Jesus that does the Augustine – Calvin – modern day you name it people who want the categories of heaven and hell to mean what they were able to glean from Dante and his ilk.

What glory can there be when we celebrate the fact that many of our earthly loved ones were not of "the elect" and are therefore burning in Hell fire? No, some do not take of their provision, so they burn in the presence of God's loving heat. The heat is the heat of God's love, a love that, in 33AD, declared that his Son was crucified for all. Now in the culmination of the ages, the crucified One still holds out the invitation. "But it's not fair! I wanted a party all along and all I had was canon law or long drawn out sermons or dull meaningless hymns or Mickey Mouse choruses without content or transcendent meaning!" Does the Father ever stop loving his "enemies?" When does God cease inviting. To cease being a God who invites, he ceases being a God of grace, and therefore is not the God revealed in Scripture.

"Enough! Enough they cry – move us along!" Okay – I did get a wee bit waylaid. What I must say is that we must be cruciform in our history, our heritage and our hope, precisely because this is what retains the power of love over all other powers and finally at the end of time as we know it, and at the point of the *telos* of God's meta-narrative, the holiness and love of God must – must be our only hope.

Many decades ago, John Henry Jowett, of whom all who are of my age and older will have heard, wrote, *"We preach Christ crucified, because it is the doctrine which incomparably preserves for us the sense of the holiness of God."*

Everything is coalesced into the cross and its provisions – into the cross and its benefits. The benefits or effects of the cruciform model are several. Christ benefits from Calvary in that he "learned obedience of the cross;" he passed through death for his entire creation; and he rose from the grave as the "Christus Victor" of the Universe of which he is King.

The cross benefits humankind, for in the Ascension, we now have a person at the right hand of God who has been "touched with the feelings of our infirmities." Jesus Christ knows how to tell the Father what we need. All that we need we find supplied either in life or in death. The Apostle Paul was convincingly clear.

In the Holy Scriptures, we see a progressive revelation from the canonical order of the Hebrew writings through the New Testament. In Abraham we have the cross over the nation, the nation which becomes Israel – God's chosen people who were to be his invitation-givers on earth; in the life of Moses, we see the cross over a household, providing a miraculous upbringing in the midst of laws that would take his life as a child. As Israel becomes a nation under Saul and then David and then Solomon, we see the cross over a faith community, for it is in the reign of King David that the Hebrews begin to leave their twelve cultic family ways and form what God would reckon as the Hebrew people: not just a nation, a people with his name. Then Jesus comes and his invitations are individual: "follow me..." and these invitations are the cross over the individual: the Father, through the Son inviting prodigals home. Finally, the church is seen in The Revelation to John as the bride of Christ and the symbol of eternality is a marriage supper. This is the cross over creation; the new creation wherein resides righteousness. Nothing does us more good than to see the cross defining what God is doing from "before the foundation of the world" through to the "even so Lord Jesus come" in the closing of The Revelation to John. And in Jesus' high priestly prayer of John chapter 17, he tells the Father, "I am glorified in them...." Who is the "them?" The "them" is us. We must now think about this. Amen.

Chapter Eighteen
Cruciformity Confirmed

Scholars, by and large, wish to discover something new, unique, never-before-seen. It is how they secure their PhD or ThD or some other terminal academic degree. This author has done it three times – and if you wish to see me brag – you will have a long wait. What I have most discovered has been through the cross not through a curriculum. I do not diminish the help a good education can be and many can afford them. But I was born into, and raised in, and ministered below the poverty level. I took what education I could find and secured degrees along the way. All of them are legitimate, a few of them are 'accredited" which means some small group of people approved another school to do what they say they are doing. Accreditation is not all that it is cracked up to be, believe me. I've seen it through from both sides now, and still somehow, it has a faint odor of self-congratulations to it.

How did we get that far a field? We got off subject because of the other way to learn – technical and secular as over and against spiritual and cruciform.

In 1989 this author published *Christ's Centripetal Cross*. I mention this to let my readership know that I think I discovered this way of sanctification early, and published it before a colleague who has done the same, with much more academic substance and aplomb. I honor Michael J. Gorman for his new work, *Inhabiting the Cruciform God: Kenosis, Justification, and Theosis in Paul's Narrative Soteriology*. This, based on a previous publication in 2001, was released in 2009. So I merely point out that Gorman confirms that I was possibly onto something in the 1980s. It was the decade when I was an inner city pastor and then a pastor in the most prestigious suburb of a Southern city where I was dismissed as pastor for "bringing those kind" into the church. It was a reference to my integrating the parish. I also suffered at the hands of a Board of Elders in a northern suburban church – a Board of upper middle class prigs who saw spirituality through modernist scientific naturalistic glasses and were not interested in the cruciform spirituality through which God was dragging me. God dragged me into this and in the process the Board of Elders stabbed me repeatedly in the back – all the while the church grew. If it were not for God's cruciformity I would commend the entire bunch of the elders to eternal fire (which is even becoming a difficult belief for me in any simple exposition). So I beat Dr. Gorman to press. Dr. Gorman beats me to the mind of this truth. I am drawn to and deeply appreciative of his book. And I trust he will not be too upset with me for taking a few quotes from his Introduction.

He begins by quoting his friend and my acquaintance and former summer school mentor, N. T. Wright who writes, "As every serious reader of Paul has long recognized, though not so many have explored to the full, the cross of Jesus the Messiah stands at the heart of Paul's vision of the one true God" (from *Paul: In Fresh Perspective*). Gorman then continues in his own words:

> *The logical corollary of this claim – a claim with which I heartily agree – is that an experience of the cross, a spirituality of the cross, is also an experience and spirituality of God – and vice versa....*
>
> *For Paul, God is cruciform. If that is true, then cruciformity is really theoformity or, as the Christian tradition (especially in the East) has sometimes called it, deification, divinization, or theosis. It is conformity to Christ, or holiness, understood as participation in the very life of God – inhabiting the cruciform God....*
>
> *"Philippians 2:6-11, which may be called Paul's master story, to show that Christ's kenosis (self-emptying) reveals the character of God, summoning us to cruciformity understood as theosis....(According to Galatians 2:15-21 and Romans 6:1-7:6) justification is by co-crucifixion; it is participation in the covenential and cruciform*

167

narrative identity of Christ, which is in turn the character of God; thus justification is itself theosis....For Paul, holiness is redefined as participation in and conformity to the cruciform character of the triune God, Father, Son, and Spirit. Holiness is not a supplement to justification but the actualization of justification, and may be more appropriately termed theosis."

Thank you, Dr. Gorman, for confirming what I saw in pastoral theology in 1989. *Solo Deo Gloria!*

Chapter Nineteen
An Afterward from a Place
I Would Never Have Expected

This Afterward was not part of the original intent of this book whatsoever. But truth is truth and, if Jesus Christ is "Truth" then Truth itself must be as infinite and eternal as the Christ, himself. We can certainly agree on that syllogism, I trust. So there is always, and will always be more Truth to be coming forth from that Fount of Truth forevermore.

After the first proof of this was returned to me, I completed the reading of Phyllis Tickle's book, *The Great Emergence: How Christianity is Changing and Why.* I was supremely disturbed by the concept of a "changing" Christianity but gave her the benefit of the doubt and took up her book.

First, I must report that her brief take on the history and present state of Christianity, particularly in the West is beyond equal. Her insights are thorough; her evaluations fair; and her vision of consequence is clear and focused. The book through that point alone was worth the purchase price.

But as I read along, I came to page 134, almost the end of the book. Now please remember that my original *Christ's Centripetal Cross* was released in 1989 and Ms. Tickle is writing to be published in 2008, nineteen years later. I was dumbfounded by what I found. It was a wonderful series of moments as I read and re-read pages 134 and 135 before moving on.

Two important things should be brought together, however in my inclusion of Ms. Tickle's references. First, I can only adopt what she says, because I believe there is a deeper and more rich and full version of it in the writings of Pierre Teilhard de Chardin, and he convinced me two dozen years ago that centripetal reality was the culmination of the age in the Christic center—the Omega Point, which is nothing more or less than the Lord Jesus Christ taking up all things into himself in the recreation of the heavens and the earth. The new creation and the party, the marriage supper of the Lamb, will be the end, the *telos* of all things—when everything is reconciled to God and God to all things because of the work of the Incarnate Christ.

The second matter, is that I believe Ms. Tickle plays closer to the edge than I would in allowing the less-than-serious dealings with the simple, few, but still very miraculous verities concerning the Christ, Incarnate in the person of Jesus of Nazareth. She does not dwell on this for a long period, but her identification with and undo emphasis on "progressive" Christianity makes one a bit wary. I merely say this as this is a personal concern. And I do set it off to the side to grasp the view of the centripetal nature of the coming Eschaton (though I believe she may have difficulty with my use of that word). Essentially, Ms. Tickle is the progressive Christian and Mackey is the traditionalist in her schema of quadrants and ellipses—and I am comfortable remaining there since she includes me in this grand scheme of future things.

Remaining well in the use of the term, concept and reality of Christianity, Tickle writes,

> American religion had never had a center before, primarily because it was basically Protestant in its Christianity; and Protestantism, with its hallmark characteristic of divisiveness, had never had a center. Now one was emerging, but what was emerging was no longer Protestant. It was no longer any "thing" actually. It was simply itself, a mélange of "things" cherry-picked from each quadrant (you'll have to read the book) and put together—some would say cobbled together—without any original intention and certainly with no design beyond that of conversation....
>
> There is enormous energy in centripetal force, especially as it gathers more and more of its own kind into itself. Centripetal force, though, is usually envisioned by us running downward, like water in a bathtub drain. The gathering force of the new Christianity

did the opposite. It ran upward and poured itself out, like some bursting geyser, in expanding waves of influence and nourishment. Where once the corners had met, now there was a swirling center, its centripetal force racing from quadrant to quadrant in ever-widening circles, picking up ideas and people from each, sweeping them into the center, mixing them there, and then spewing them forth into a new way of being Christian, into a new way of being Church....

The whole progression from distinct corners to a gathering center was precisely and exactly what sociologists and observers of religion had predicted would happen....(And may I add, so does the Canon of Holy Scripture).[6]

Would not Teilhard be excited? Should we not all be beyond expectant that God who is "the propitiation for our sins," is "not for ours only, but for the sins of the whole world?" Should we not be somehow at a centripetal peace knowing that the Prince of Peace is drawing his crowd?

---

[6] Phyllis Tickle, *The Great Emergence: How Christianity is Changing and Why,* Grand Rapids, MI: Baker Books, 2008, 134-135.

Bibliography

The following bibliography is but a necessary introduction to a study of the Cross of Christ. Please refer to it before you begin to study some of the twenty-first century theories of the cross which will have no deep meaning to you until you can read them in the context of Scripture and tradition. By including these books in the Bibliography this author does not mean to indicate that he agrees with all the author writes.

Forsyth, P. T. *The Cruciality of the Cross.* n.c.: Kessinger Publishing Company. 2006.

Goudge, H. L. *Glorying in the Cross.* London: Hodder & Stoughton. 1940.

Green, Joel B. and Mark D. Baker. *Recovering the Scandal of the Cross: Atonement in New Testament and Contemporary Contexts.* Downers Grove, IL: Inter Varsity Press, 2000.

Heim, S. Mark. *Saved from Sacrifice: A Theology of the Cross.* Grand Rapids, MI: Eerdmans. 2006.

Horton, Michael. *Christless Christianity: The Alternative Gospel of the American Church.* Grand Rapids, MI: Baker Books. 2008.

Lloyd-Jones, Martyn, *The Cross: God's Way of Salvation.* New York: Crossroads. 1986.

Millard, T. L. *Foolishness to the Greeks.* Greenwich, CT: Seabury Books. 1853.

Miller, Calvin. *Once Upon a Tree.* West Monroe, LA: Howard Publishing Company. 2002

Neumann, R. *The Cross of Golgotha: Lenten and Passiontide Mediations and Sermons.* Burlington, IA: The Lutheran Literary Board. 1926.

Sell, Alan P. F. *Confessing and Commending the Faith: Prolegomena to Christian Apologetics.* Eugene, OR: Wipf & Stock Publishers. 2002.

Sheen, Fulton J. *The Cross and the Crisis.* Milwaukee, WI: The Bruce Publishing Company. 1938.

Stott, John R. W. *The Cross of Christ.* Downers Grove, IL: Inter Varsity Press. 2006.

Tozer, A. W. *The Cross: Living the Passion of Christ.* Camp Hill, PA: Wingspread Publishers. 2009.

_____. *Who Put Jesus on the Cross?* Camp Hill, PA: Wingspread Publishers, 2009.

Tickle, Phyllis. *The Great Emergence: How Christianity is Changing and Why.* Grand Rapids, MI: Baker Books. 2008.

von Balthasar, Hans Urs. *The Way of the Cross.* Middlegreed, Slough: England. 1990.

The Wilson Press

Dr. Henry Wilson, a Canadian Anglican clergyman was convincingly directed by his late nineteenth century Protestant/liberal bishop to break all ties he had formed with the very aggressive and evangelistic Salvation Army. This broke Henry Wilson's heart.

Through a great number of correspondences with Bishop Potter of the Diocese of New York, and by invitation of the very well-known Dr. Rainsford, Wilson was invited to be the Associate Rector at St. George's Parish in New York City. He took up the work with great resolve and soon was a beloved clergyman throughout the city. Wilson again made friends with the Salvation Army, and with anyone else who would be interested in the simple Gospel message.

Dr. Rainsford, of St. Georges, had already begun to establish himself as a leader in the "Institutional Church" movement, a movement which involved, usually larger churches, in the work of Gospel preaching and social justice. St. Georges was a hub of nonstop activity for God. Biblical ecumenicity was being practiced.

Onto the scene came a Presbyterian named Albert B. Simpson, better known simply as A. B. Simpson. He and Rainsford became friends and Rainsford introduced Simpson to his Associate Henry Wilson. An inseparable friendship was formed, and later, after Wilson's death, Simpson called him, "One of God's best!"

So Wilson was an early cross-over visionary. There have been few. The mainline has looked with disdain on the

177

free-church evangelicals while the evangelicals have looked on the mainline congregations as Gospel-lacking, hell-deserving dinosaurs. Each is wrong, by the way, and Wilson would have had none of it!

The Wilson Press is committed to the publication of books by men and women of God who have no agenda but God's agenda and that is the preaching of the Gospel of Jesus Christ. There are few books to date, but the number will grow as commitment to denominational formality wanes in light of a growing and spreading Biblical ecumenicity once more in the twenty-first century. Enjoy your book from Wilson Press.

The Publisher

Made in the USA
Charleston, SC
16 September 2011